Resilience
A PERSON, NOT JUST A PATIENT

Angela McCrimmon

Aurora Books
Eugene, Oregon, USA

Copyright © 2022 Angela McCrimmon

All rights reserved. No part of this book may be reproduced or transmitted in any form or by any means electronic or mechanical including photocopying, recording, or by any information storage and retrieval system without permission in writing from the publisher.

Aurora Books, an imprint of Eco-Justice Press, L.L.C.

Aurora Books
P.O. Box 5409 Eugene, OR 97405
www.ecojusticepress.com

Resilience: A Person, Not Just a Patient
By Angela McCrimmon

Cover by Eco-Justice Press

Library of Congress Control Number: 2022941557

ISBN 978-1-945432-51-4

This book is dedicated to my dearly missed Mother and Father. The biggest legacy they have left behind is their children and I intend to honour that legacy by remembering the love and laughter we shared and to strive to be the kind of person that even from the heavens above, they will look down and say, "That's Our Girl." I will miss them forever but the gratitude I have of being lucky enough to have had them at all, and for as long as I did will always bring me comfort.

Until We Meet Again…..

John Rae   16/08/1950 – 02/11/2019

Joyce Rae 09/02/1954 – 06/03/2022

XXX

Table of Contents

Introduction………7

1 - The Complexity Of My Mind………11

2 - Our Lives, Their Hands………31

3 - My Recipe For Wellbeing………55

4 - Life In Lockdown………77

5 - Family Forever………93

Introduction

When I wrote, "Can You Hear Me Now? Finding My Voice In a System That Stole It, " I certainly never envisaged a consequent book of poems emerging to allow me to continue to share my journey with you. Even more surprising is that I definitely didn't think that this book would be a book full of hope, to allow the readers to see that my experience in the Health Care System actually did improve. The years between my first book and this book have brought me a new Psychiatrist and General Practitioner who work consistently alongside me to help me have the best quality of life possible. There's no getting away from the fact that Bipolar Disorder is an unpredictable illness so it's still been a bit of a rollercoaster ride, but these days I don't feel like I'm riding it alone. Where once there was no hope and I was so severely misunderstood, I find myself today helping people who are part of my care to understand me better so that they have the full picture of what they are treating. The difference now is that they are open to listening to my thoughts and ideas of what I feel will help me most. Of course I understand that they will always have the final decision on any treatment or diagnosis and I respect that. I've been in the Mental Health System for 26 years and I feel it's only been in the last 6 years I've actually felt that respect working both ways. It's incredibly important in a Therapeutic Relationship to feel there is genuine mutual respect. In the previous years when I was scared into silence, my coping skills still earned me a reputation of "attention seeking." So, I decided that if they were going to think this of me anyway then I might as well speak up and get some 'attention,' - but not just for myself. I wanted to speak up for anyone else out there who hadn't yet found their own voice.

I've learned a lot about myself because the last few years have seen me dealing with some hugely heart-breaking and challenging things. I've often thought someone should make my life into a movie and then I have the sad realisation that it's actually so unbelievable, people would struggle to believe that it's true. Nothing about me or my life is ordinary and while I love that exciting opportunities always come my way, it also leaves me wondering what on earth is going to happen next. The thing I learned most about myself is how brave and resilient I am. Yes, I know people tell me I'm brave every day to get up and engage in a world that paralyzes me with anxiety at times but when I say brave, I mean REALLY brave.

I finally found the courage to go through a Medical Tribunal against a Dr who abused his position of trust 26 years ago and I believe he did so on the basis that I was a mental health patient so if I ever spoke up, nobody would believe me. 20 years later and an utterly horrific 17hour cross-examination by the Doctor's Barrister, eventually brought about the verdict of Guilty! He was subsequently struck off and removed from the medical register. I... WAS... BELIEVED. Any mental health patient will know the power of this statement. I had carried this trauma for so many years because I, too, believed that with 20 years of often detrimental Psychiatric Notes against me, who was ever going to believe me? This process wasn't about the outcome for me, it was about simply having the courage to finally speak up for what was right. The re-traumatisation of the experience was beyond description but I don't regret for one minute that I finally had him held accountable by the General Medical Council for things that a) should never have happened and b) probably subconsciously set me up for a lifetime of mistrusting the Medical Profession.

It seems surreal to even write this but sadly since my last book, both my Mother and Father have passed away. This had the potential to unravel my mental health in a heartbeat. However, using a lot of the well-being tools I share with you in Chapter 3, I knew that I could either drown in the grief of losing the 2 people I loved most in the world or I could choose to pick myself up and carry on living life in their honour. Everyone copes with grief differently and I absolutely respect this but for me, the loss of my parents has only re-enforced my appreciation of life and it's fragility. I want to make the most of every moment. I want to watch the sunrise, I want to have adventures, I want to cherish and nourish relationships, I want to contribute to the lives of others and areas of life that I'm passionate about……but above everything, I want to make memories and to be able to make those memories my mental health has to feel stable and supported. I work as hard as I can on my part to take responsibility for keeping myself "well" and I finally feel that my Doctors work with me, not against me, with the common goal of my mental health being the best it can be.

Since writing "Can You Hear Me Now? Finding My Voice In A System That Stole It," I have had the privilege of having my voice heard on many different platforms. I have written poems and articles for many different organisations, including quite regularly, the International Bipolar Foundation. I've taken part in National Media Campaigns to help combat Stigma and Discrimination and I've even popped up on Television and Radio a few times to fight my cause. My proudest moment was recently being asked to share some of my experience in Scottish Parliament to 17 different organisations who had come together to make up the Scottish Mental Health Partnership to promote a Government Manifesto of "Promote, Prevent, Provide," as they undertake the enormous task of coming up with new Strategy to support people and their mental health with all the complexities of post-covid added into the mix. If you read my last book, did you ever imagine in a million years that I would be consistently well enough to enjoy, engage and accept these opportunities to contribute to the future of Mental Health Services?

One of the biggest keys to my resilience is Gratitude. Rather than focus on what I've lost in life, I make a very conscious effort to focus on what I still have in the here and now. So much of life is about perspective and I think to cope with my illness I have literally trained my brain to find the good in even horrendous situations…..because if you look hard enough, I guarantee you'll find something. What could I find good about losing my parents I hear you wonder? Of course I'm heartbroken to lose them, but how lucky was I to have them at all and for as long as I did? How lucky was I that my Mum was my best friend in the world? Not everyone has that special relationship with their Mother but I recognise how lucky I was that I can honestly say our relationship was so very precious. I will be forever grateful for what I do have rather than obsess over what was taken away. That grasp of Gratitude that I hold onto throughout every day of my life, I believe is a huge part of what gives me the strength to pick myself back up after anything sends me crashing to the ground.

I have too much to be grateful for to give up now.

1
The Complexity Of My Mind

"The brain gives the heart it's sight, the heart gives the brain it's vision
– Rob Kall

    Our minds are complex creatures and that's before we add in a mental illness or any life events that might shape the way we think and see the world. Having layers of complexity makes life more challenging but I'm so proud that despite having this illness, I still show up for life and give it my best shot. That takes courage. I have only recently come to acknowledge how much bravery I show in both my every day life and in some of the extraordinary experiences I've lived through. I have learned so much about myself in the last few years and I love that because my brain is "complex," I have a deep rooted love and desire for learning. I've always found that I can calm the chaos in my mind if I can understand where the storm has come from. Sometimes I have to unravel all that complexity and break it into bite size pieces to digest in a way that won't overwhelm my mind. I like that my mind is complex as it allows me to see things from every perspective possible……but it's also exhausting. I wouldn't wish to be any other way, but my hope would be that Health Professionals would be able to identity this, develop an understanding for me as an individual, and maybe even welcome the complexity of my mind as a tool they can learn from.

Priceless

I have good self-awareness, and I practice good self-care,
I monitor my mood but there was a piece missing there,
The piece about anxiety and where it all begins,
I try to push on through but the anxiety always wins.

You'll tell me, "that's life," we can all feel this way,
For me it's more extreme, I'll tell you if I may,
When the anxiety is physical and it's crawling on my skin,
I hurt myself to stop it, it's been my only way to win.

It's effective but I know that things will have to change,
I've tried so many things but there are none that I'd exchange,
Then one day I realised that I knew I held the key,
All these years the solution was deep inside of me.

I have to find a way to stop anxiety in its track,
When my stomach starts to churn, it's telling me turn back,
Where usually I'd always try to fight it with such force,
I'll say "hello anxiety," then cut if off at source.

I don't want to be unreliable, but if I have to be I will,
I like my life fast-paced, but if I have to I'll stand still,
I made myself a promise so from now on I won't think twice,
If something costs me my peace then it isn't worth the price.

Back To Life

My curtains are closed to block the world out,
But I can still hear the falling rain,
It's almost like it is trying to shout,
"Hey, get back out here again!!"

It seems I'd taken my eye off of the ball,
Thinking "just one day in bed,"
I didn't predict how hard I'd fall,
That it would end up a week instead.

The trouble is that when I feel like this,
The very worst thing I could do,
Is cancel my plans, appointments I miss,
Then retreat and withdraw from you.

I tell myself each day and each night,
As I lie there and toss and turn,
Maybe tomorrow will be alright?
You'd think by now I would learn.

I feel motivation wash over me,
Then no sooner it's gone down the drain,
I'm praying that I will be able to see,
Tomorrow might not be the same.

A Bad Day....And That's Okay!

"Keep things in perspective," often my self-talk,
I preach the revelation but do I walk the walk?
When my days are long and I'm feeling rather tired,
Could I be a little prone to some catastrophise?

I used to wake up early and literally hold my breath,
To be honest each day I was often scared to death,
So frightened of whichever mood that I might feel,
Knowing my emotions would feel so raw and real.

It scared me to realise that I could go to sleep,
Quite happily with many nice memories to keep,
The chemicals in my brain could have their own merry dance,
And where they landed next day was purely luck and chance.

If I woke up feeling anxious or with effort overload,
I'd panic and be scared of this old familiar road,
Weeks of depression where I could barely interact,
Then one day it hit me.....it didn't have to be a fact!

I could have a "bad day," just like the universe,
It doesn't mean I'm getting ill or that my life is cursed,
I don't panic anymore or overthink my strife,
A "bad day" doesn't mean that I'm having a "bad life."

<u>Recovery</u>

Self-harm taught me a lesson that was very hard to learn,
So valuable however, it taught me to discern,
Between "being in recovery" or "being totally recovered,"
A bitter pill to swallow when this I first discovered.

I truly thought I'd left self-destruction far behind,
I thought I'd escaped from that part of my mind,
A few years had passed with barely any urge,
But it came back like a hunger, a binge and then a purge.

I'd sometimes reflect and wonder deep inside,
How I'd coped with the wounds I always had to hide,
The irony being that I don't even like 'normal' pain,
Yet it's a place I found myself back in once again.

"Relapse" is a word I try not to use,
Is it really an "addiction" of self-abuse?
I use the word "blip" though I know I underplay,
The severity of the actual real cost that I pay.

I guess the lesson that I learned the most,
If I'm winning the battle I'll never boast,
For with that battle I'll have to choose,
Sometimes I'll win and sometimes I'll lose.

Insomnia In A Nutshell

The nights are long when I cannot sleep,
When the sunset and the sunrise meet,
My head races and I'm agitated,
Medicated yet not sedated.
I feel myself rocking to and fro,
As if to soothe myself I know,
Anxiety builds when overtired,
Exhausted yet simultaneously wired,
These hours have many a story to tell,
Insomnia is like a waking hell!

Mania

I feel my energy start to rise,
The mania dances in my eyes,
My thoughts and speech will start to race,
Other struggle to keep the pace.
My enthusiasm will overwhelm,
My reality's in a whole new realm,
My thoughts are fast, you can't keep up,
In conversations I interrupt.
Little sleep or none at all,
I aim so high, no fear to fall,
My filter seems to go astray,
There's no guessing what I'm going to say.
Can't concentrate, distracted thoughts,
I left the house, my skirt forgot!
Friends and family can't sustain,
Tell me I'm making them go insane,
The Dr calls, we both agree,
It's a medication tweak for me.
I hear so many people say,
"I'd love to be you....just for a day,"
Behind my smile I want to tell,
"Too happy" still means that I'm unwell.

Glass Half Empty

Is your glass half empty or is your glass half full?
Maybe you are drowning in a swimming pool?
Life observations are truly the key,
Of making real sense of life for me.

There can be 2 friends looking at an identical view,
Yet so many differences it cannot be true,
The difference it seems is not what they see,
It's how they internalise that picture to be.

Are you prone to always seeing the downside to life?
Influenced by somewhat struggle and strife,
Or do you see the world as a gift to treasure?
The sun shines strong, no matter the weather.

I've found that to add to my life being good,
It's crucial I practice daily gratitude,
I might not yet be where I visualise me,
But thank god I'm not where I used to be.

Is your glass half empty or is your glass half full?
I guess my friends, there is one golden rule,
Whether it's overflowing or down to nil,
Your glass can always be refilled.

Apology Letter

I am who I am, I can only be me,
An empowering statement that set me free,
No impossible standards to live up to,
Seeing through the eyes that some others do.

I stopped comparing myself to the world,
I accepted I was a bright and beautiful girl,
Because beauty begins from the inside out,
I had an inner beauty, no need to shout.

I have talents and skills I never gave credit,
Whatever I wrote, I'd spend hours to edit,
So sure that somehow I "must do better,"
Until one day I wrote myself an apology letter.....

"Dear Me,

I'm sorry that I often pass you by,
I don't acknowledge how hard you try,
I push you on to always try your best,
When sometimes what you need is to rest.
I'm sorry I compare you with others around,
You're an individual with your cause to be found,
You have so much passion that it scares me even,
For I think you're an unstoppable force to believe in!
I cause you to doubt but let me say it's true,
I think you'll be amazing at whatever you do,
I say this because you live from your heart,
Prove the doubters wrong and blow their theories apart."

So there we have it in black and white,
My subconscious telling me we're ready to fight,
Ready to go to battle together,
And ready to win, whatever the weather.

Please let me make this point very clear,
These battles are only with myself here,
I know that one day I will win the war,
And I'll wonder what on earth the fighting was for.

Trauma Informed Care

When you have a mental illness it doesn't leave much room,
To express an emotion without it being assumed,
That somehow you're being irrational, dramatic to the core,
But what they are not seeing, is what has gone before.

I experience anxiety and I know that it's profound,
But for years I held my silence, too afraid to make a sound,
To function in the world parts of me detached,
All I ask is for some kindness as I fight to get them back.

I hadn't even realised that I lived in such a way,
I was flooding my nervous system every single day,
We all need "fight or flight" in an occasional healthy dose,
But for me it consumed my body, living in "survival mode."

You see certain behaviours and more labels then appear,
"Just attention seeking" is the one that holds most fear,
For with this assumption I'm so misunderstood,
I'm not looking for "attention" but the irony is I should!

I know I'm very complex but therein lies the key,
It tells you there is much more than meets the eye to me,
Trauma leaves it's mark and what I need from you,
Is sensitivity and wisdom as I try to work it through.

Introvert Under Cover

It's easy to assume that I'm quite the extrovert,
But I'm really on a mission, the kind that is covert,
My mission is to play my part, in hope you cannot tell,
I'm so far out my comfort zone, it feels like I'm in hell.

Every fibre of my being just loves to be alone,
For decades I had a phobia of speaking on the phone,
I couldn't listen to a voicemail, I collected quite a stack,
I was so scared that the caller may request I call them back!

I'm aware that I feel 'different' but 'lonely' isn't true,
I don't crave people's company the way most others do,
I do love many people but it's always been the same,
Any lengthy interaction just leaves me feeling drained.

I love to play my music and listen to audiobooks,
I get so absorbed in projects that food gets overlooked,
Give me a documentary and I'll hang on every word,
Give me real conversation and I feel like I'm disturbed.

I travel many places and solo is just fine,
Less effort is required for it doesn't tire my mind,
I feel like an impostor when I walk into a room,
I've logged off in such a panic from many calls on Zoom!

I deeply care for others so I'm not a sociopath!
I definitely have a conscience, so we can cross off any of that,
It's like I just don't 'fit' but I've trained myself so well,
I force myself to function so that nobody can tell.

So next time you see me standing up there on a stage,
Or if you read the newspaper and I stare up from the page,
This doesn't make me "extrovert," I'm just trying my very best,
To merge with it the "introvert," so I can be just like the rest.

Angela McCrimmon

People-Pleasing

We're the first to offer, it's just who we are,
Even if it's inconvenient too,
Our "people-pleasing" nature is never very far,
Because let's face it.....it's what we do.

We're taught to think of others but we've taken the extreme,
It didn't mean that this should be at our expense,
Putting ourselves last isn't ever what they mean,
"But I like to help," was always my defence.

I had to learn the lesson of who was worth my time,
Ultimately, who actually cared for me?
If I had needed help there was never any line,
Reaching for my hand that I could see.

I have to make it clear that I do not give to get,
I don't need repaying of any kind,
But if I don't reach out to you then please don't forget,
Maybe let me know I'm on your mind?

I've come a long way with the "people-pleasing" trait,
The first person I must please is myself,
I'll still try to help but there are times you'll have to wait,
If I'm already doing something else.

If helping you out will drain everything I've got,
My self-care says, "Sorry, no can do,"
I finally learned that I am not an afterthought,
And my own needs are so important too.

Loyalty

My body has endured what most will never see,
And yet it has shown incredible loyalty to me,
A loyalty I didn't ask for, let alone deserve,
I was fighting to destroy while it was fighting to preserve.

I didn't harm through hate, it wasn't self-esteem,
It was the physical anxiety that made me want to scream,
Skin crawling, heart racing, digestion upside down,
My self-harm screamed STOP!.. and these things would settle down.

It took the last episode to make me understand,
It's an absolute miracle I haven't lost my arm,
The damage I have done is like nothing I've done before,
But it's the one that's made me say, "I don't want to do this anymore!"

I wish I'd had this fright so many years ago,
Nothing seemed to scare me, even if a limb should go,
To stop the anxiety I was willing to take the chance,
For decades my body and insanity in a dance.

I know I can't proclaim that self-harm is gone for good,
I hope it won't return but I'm well aware it could,
I'm saying sorry to my body and thank you for being so strong,
Somehow you kept us safe, and together where we belong.

Dreams

Do you ever have those nights when you have a million dreams,
You wonder what on earth each one could ever mean?
They say that when we dream it's our brain's filing system,
I think my office junior deserves worldwide recognition!!

I woke up a million times and wrote upon some paper,
For I knew I had no chance of remembering it later,
The first dream I awoke from really made me laugh,
I was off on a Safari, riding a giraffe??

I tried to fall asleep as I closed my eyes with laughter,
To waken once again, not more than one hour after,
This time I had dreamed I was involved in some crazy crime,
I think I'll need to monitor what I watch before bedtime!

I closed my eyes once more, and thought of the day ahead,
Concerned that I'd fall asleep when I should be getting up instead,
This time I went back to childhood as my brain somehow recalled,
The day I got ready for school when there was no school at all!

I looked at my alarm clock and the time was 05.03,
In less than just one hour it would be singing out to me,
I use the word "singing" because it's set to my favourite song,
It blasts out when it's still dark in the hope I'll sing along.

So here I am awake now but what a busy night!
A different dream each hour, surely that can't be right?
No wonder I find myself tired as I carry out my day,
My "filing system" operator will be demanding extra pay!

Time To Take My Own Advice

You're so quick with compassion when others are in need,
Slow down for yourself, pull back on the speed.
The patience you show in such a natural way,
I'd like you to be most patient with yourself today.
Your energy and enthusiasm for being alive,
Take your ideas and allow them to thrive.
Be selective of who you choose in your "tribe,"
Trust your gut feelings, you'll sense the vibe.
You're quick to help out and give others your time,
I want you to pause, re-adjust, re-align.
Interaction exhausts you so you need to plug in,
To extra self-care - recharge from within.
Boundaries aren't just for "professional" states,
Set them right now and see who will wait.
I've kept you together, healed your body each time,
Please never again, this line was too fine.
You'd never hurt others so I'm begging you please,
Stop hurting ME now and set our soul free.

Embodiment of Anxiety

I don't think anxious thoughts and I don't catastrophise,
Assumptions that are made but mistaken otherwise,
For the anxiety I feel is not from conscious mind,
I feel it in my body, it's an all-consuming kind.

My head holds onto logic but it just does not extend,
To stop my stomach churning, the message doesn't send,
There's no threat in my vision or warnings up ahead,
But my body feels in danger as it sinks in such deep dread.

I approach you with a smile but what you cannot see,
Is the fear inside my soul when I know there need not be,
My fingers start to tingle as my nerves just come alive,
Adrenaline courses through my veins helping it to thrive.

My brain doesn't seem to relax or turn off to fall asleep,
It's like there's a secret switch which I don't know where I keep,
I'm in a medicated coma just to get me through the night,
Some relief at last but it comes at such a price.

I've tried so many things and I'll try so many more,
I'll never give up trying to break down my own door,
It's not my cognition running wild in my thoughts,
"My body keeps the score," even if my memory does not.

Being Me

I live my world with routine so when life takes that away,
It steals my place of safety and I struggle through each day,
I lose all that's familiar and my life feels under threat,
I'm hanging by a thread, and I haven't lost it.......yet!

People see the "product" of my very strict regime,
To them I function well and they won't know what I mean,
But if they could step into my shoes for even just one day,
I think they'd be surprised at my many million ways....

.....Ways to cope with this, or ways to cope with that,
Things they'll take for granted will leave me in a flap,
A simple conversation can leave me in a spin,
If I haven't had the chance to prepare for it within.

If my day had expectations and places I should be,
If that changes in a moment, this change distresses me,
I don't mean I get angry, it's not that kind of pain,
It's simply "overwhelm"....I don't cope well with change.

My head does a rehearsal of how my day will be,
It helps control the anxiety that lives inside of me,
It plans out each manoeuvre so that I'm prepared,
Unexpected movement leaves me feeling scared.

So when you look at me and think, "wow, she's so together,"
Pause for just a moment to question if it ever,
Made you stop to realise there's much more that you don't see,
And actually in reality, it's hard work being me.

Angela McCrimmon

I Am Enough

I'm creative and chaotic, I'm caring and I'm kind…
I'm mostly in control but I sometimes lose my mind.
I'm manic and depressive, and albeit this is true…
I know "I am enough," and I'll always make it through.
I'm focused and distracted, my energy runs high…
I only see a failure if I have failed to try.
I'm simple but I'm complex, a contradictive paradigm…
I know "I am enough" for my heart and head align.
I'm strong but I am gentle, empathy beyond…
My words join the dots like the lyrics of a song.
I'm emphatic but I'm silent, I finally found my voice…
I know "I am enough" for my feelings are my choice.
I'm happy and I'm sad and I'm all that's in between…
I'm honest and authentic, I say just what I mean.
I know I "overthink" but I'm peaceful in my soul…
I know "I am enough" for these things all make me whole.
I BELIEVE "I am enough," no apology required…
I BELIEVE "I am enough," no matter how my brain is wired,
I BELIEVE "I am enough" - no better, but no less…
I'm who I'm meant to be and for that I'm truly blessed.

Mistaken Identity

"I'm Bipolar" is a statement thrown up in the air,
But for me these are words I choose with great care,
They conjure an image of being up or being down,
Crippled with sadness or racing around.

"I'm Bipolar" is a statement that says it consumes,
Each part of my life like a hungry vacuum,
Of course there are times when it feels like that's true,
But there are times when I am perfectly 'normal' like you.

"I'm Bipolar" paints a picture of the person I am,
It says what I can't do, not what I can,
Portrays my personality at such extremes,
I'm not allowed to be peaceful it seems.

"I'm Bipolar" starts a story that others believe,
They know how it ends from message received,
Unless those words comes straight from me,
Don't assume it's my story you read.

"I'm Bipolar" is a phrase I'm so careful to use,
"I HAVE Bipolar" are the words that I choose,
It's not who I am, nor who I will be,
I have an illness, not the illness is me.

2
<u>Our Lives, Their Hands</u>

"A Profession where knowledge, power and heart should come together." Lifeofamedic.com

One barrier I've hit with Mental Health Professionals is a lot of them expect you to be a textbook version of your diagnosis. NEWSFLASH: We're not! Of course there will be common symptoms between patients who share the same condition but there will also be huge contrasts too. The intricacy of everything else that makes us who we are is what I feel wasn't given the place and significance that it should have had in my care over the last 26 years. We are more than a set of chemicals inside our brains. We are people with hearts, values, experiences, beliefs and personalities too. Over the last few years I believe I have received a lot of care where this has indeed been taken into consideration and it gives me hope that the Mental Health System is moving in the direction of much more Person-Centred Care and listening to the voice of the person living with the condition. After years of being scared into silence, I have found my voice and passion to create change for a system that can adapt to the Patient as opposed to the Patient being put in a box that doesn't quite fit them, but… it's "close enough." It might be close enough, but that's not good enough. The trust that Doctors require us to place in them is such a fragile thing and if the care and respect that we hope for in return isn't forthcoming, the damage that is done to the Dr-Patient relationship can be extremely traumatising for a possibly already traumatised individual. I have been lucky enough to encounter some amazing Health Professionals over the last 6 years and in this chapter I will introduce you to some of them. It's important to speak up when things are going wrong but I think it's even more important to speak up and tell them when they're getting it right so that they learn the power of how a particular approach of care was for their patient, and can replicate it to help reach someone else.

General Practitioners

I think "General Practitioners," are so overlooked,
People look to Consultants, forgetting that it took,
Time and referrals by their general Doctor,
Monitoring their symptoms just like a proctor.

I place so much value upon my "GP,"
For I know the lengths she has gone to for me,
It's like we have been on a journey together,
She knows me today now better than ever.

If I call her she knows things are really not good,
For she knows that I'm someone who does and who would,
Try every solution to solve things alone,
I've run out of options when I pick up the phone.

She's consistent and caring, she gives me her time,
I'm not scared what to say, overthinking each line,
She's compassionate but with the right mixture to be,
Practical and pragmatic, a bit like me.

She trusts that I know myself very well,
Time taught her that, what a story to tell,
Where once she was led by the powers that be,
She learned that the person to lead her was me.

I hope she knows the difference she's made,
Putting aside the old price that was paid,
She cares and encourages, supports and defends,
She walks the road with me, with all of its bends.

Care Plan Review

"I won't say much" are the words that I said,
"I'm going to try to sit back and listen instead....
For when I speak it seems I make too much sense,
And it gets me no help as a consequence!"

The event this day was my Care Plan Review,
Psychiatrist, Dr and the Practice Nurse too,
All co-ordinated to come together,
This was a first in my life forever.

I listened that day to their every word,
A lot of their views were very absurd,
I remember I was still feeling really quite low,
They thought this was my 'normal' but how could they know?

I realised they had got me even more wrong,
Just like they had in my care all along,
"Personality Disorder??"....I wanted to scream,
But I dare not for fear of what that might mean.

Instead, I made a true promise to keep,
As I realised that I held the missing piece,
I was determined that I would help them to see,
The true picture of how life is for me.

My responsibility, I took back control,
To work together, that was the goal,
That meeting truly turned my life around,
I kept my promise and my voice was found.

"Press 1 For An Emergency…..Press 2 For An Interrogation"

I hear so many stories and yet they're all the same,
"Trying to see my GP really isn't worth the pain,
I call at 8 o'clock just like they tell us to,
But it seems 3000 other Patients call then too."

I chuckle inside because I know just what they mean,
I start calling at 8am and every-time in between,
I use the key "redial," so it dials it once again,
The phone records each attempt, once 110!!

I've finally been connected, I've finally made it through,
To be told that I am maybe 5th in the queue,
As I start to get closer, I begin to feel quite sick,
My mind goes blank with panic, and it needs to come back quick!

I'm not panicking about the Dr, there's a hurdle I must leap,
I must first describe my symptoms to the Medical Practice Police,
The receptionists, who last I checked had no medical degree,
Are the ones who decide if a Dr should see me.

Some I'll stress are lovely and tho' only on a phone,
I can tell they want to help, I can hear it in their tone,
Others I can sense when they even hear my name,
They don't even try to hide, "Oh, it's her again."

I do understand that they're there to signpost,
So we see the person who can help us the most,
These days I know a nurse can do so much more,
Like prescribing things that they could never before.

I guess I just feel that I shouldn't feel scared,
Or start to panic feeling underprepared,
Worrying that my symptoms won't show I'm in need,
For if I'm calling the Dr she is needed indeed!

I can go for months with things calm and stable,
But then a crisis arrives, and I am barely able,
To pick up the phone before it's too late,
When they stand in my way, they might seal my fate.

Please know I respect you and the job that you do,
But please could I ask that you respect me too,
Maybe then I would try to reach out a bit faster,
Your compassion could help me avoid a disaster!

<u>In This Together</u>

I went to my appointment just like I always do,
Hiding a secret, I was the only one who knew,
Beneath my clothing was a wound that needed care,
I'd done everything I could to avoid going "there!"

"The Emergency Room," the place that I avoid,
So many bad experiences that left me so destroyed,
Their lack of understanding, and they made it very clear,
I've brought this on myself, I don't deserve the treatment here.

Within my appointment time I knew that I should tell,
We're open and we're honest and she knows me very well,
To hold back my secret with someone whom I trust,
Somehow felt unfair so to open up I must.

Firstly I apologised which really wasn't needed,
I briefly reconsidered but then my heart conceded,
She looked at me softly with compassion in her eyes,
"We need to deal with this," but she didn't criticise.

I knew how to manage this, I had a plan prepared,
After this appointment I'd go tho' feeling scared,
I felt such dread and my Doctor seen it too,
She suggested gently, "Shall I walk down with you?"

At first I declined, I must sort this out alone,
It was my responsibility and I'd do it on my own,
But when she asked again, I couldn't disagree,
We would sort this out together…my Psychiatrist and me.

We walked along the corridors where so many had before,
She kept the pace beside me as the wound was very sore,
We didn't need to talk, communication was so clear,
She walked right by my side and diminished all my fear.

She told me to sit down and vanished through a door,
She tried to help the staff understand a little more,
She emerged back towards me and mouthed "You'll be okay,"
I thanked her through my tears but I had so much to say.

I wanted to say "Thank you," for being so very calm,
No shock or disappointment in the person that I am,
"My job is to protect you," she'd said some years before,
Today I felt she'd done that….and yet done so much more.

She hadn't "reacted," but surely did "respond,"
To help me that day she went above and beyond,
She cared I got the help that my body did demand,
In facing it together, I felt her hold my hand.

Angela McCrimmon

The Story Of A Blue Glove

It wasn't my usual Dr but he stood there in the door,
"I'm here to assess you," and didn't say much more,
He had no pen and paper, so outside from a stand,
He took a surgical glove and wrote upon his hand.

He didn't ask me questions, I could feel him just assume,
"When I met Angela she was watching telly in her room,"
What a flippant observation and just because the "telly's" on,
Certainly doesn't mean that nothing else is wrong!

No respect at all, he insulted my Consultant too,
"She's on a cocktail of medication," were the words of which he used,
How dare he judge her treatment when she has taken time,
To find out what medications will help this brain of mine!

He really was creative because for all one glove of blue,
He created 2 whole pages that I could read to you,
There's just one more "quotation" that I am going to share,
I shiver to even think I was ever in this Dr's care.

I was reading this "letter" and it was about 3 lines down,
I paused for a moment and my face began to frown,
I can't seriously have read what I think that he has written,
The pain hit my heart as if I had just been bitten.

"Angela has relapsed into her familiar sick role,"
Implying I was "acting," it cut right through my soul,
"Enjoying the attention" were the words between the lines,
So arrogant and ignorant, yet he thought his care was fine.

To see him be so flippant and his words be so unkind,
Shows the danger of some Doctors "assessing" my mind,
Who'd have thought a glove of blue could cause me so much pain,
I just pray that our paths will never cross again.

A Place of Safety

You're asking me these questions, I'm begging you to see,
The answers that are hidden deep down inside of me,
My vocabulary's frozen, my voice has all but gone,
But if you look a little harder you will see that something's wrong.

I'm finding it so difficult to look you in the eye,
I'm fighting back the tears for I don't want to cry,
I'm nervous and unsettled, I'm caught in fight or flight,
A "Survival Mode" perfected but I'm flying out of sight.

You assume the medication maybe needs a little tweak,
My silent voice is screaming "Please just let me speak,"
For once it's not the chemicals dancing all around,
It's the trauma deep inside that's longing to be found.

See past what I accomplish, See past what I achieve,
For this is the Imposter that lives inside of me,
The one who can convince you that everything is fine,
When slowly and so secretively I'm losing all my mind.

I don't seek more medication for it serves as just a token,
A band aid for my heart that is tired and truly broken,
What I need is a safe place where I can finally reveal,
Please give my broken heart a safe place to heal.

Pardon?

I'll never forget the Dr's expression,
"I don't think you've ever suffered depression,"
I desperately tried to think I'd misheard.
Had they missed the parts where I longed to be dead??

I looked in their eyes because I had no words,
To say such a thing seemed so very absurd,
I thought of the times I closed my front door,
Cut off for months, my heart hit the floor.

I felt so defeated, how do I disprove?
A steadfast opinion they might not remove,
Should I be sorry that right now I'm healthy and strong?
But that doesn't mean that nothing was wrong!

When I think of the weeks rolled up in a ball,
The months I had no interaction at all,
Friends would call but they soon moved on,
The friend they knew was a friend now gone.

No interest in things that sparked me alive,
Can't call on my toolkit from which I survive,
I'm not depressed at this date and time,
But how dare they deny this illness of mine.

When they said those words I looked in their eyes,
A desperate plea that they'd hear my cries,
My soul crashed down and my heart hit the floor,
Dismissed, disbelieved, and unheard once more.

Her Laugh Should Be On Prescription!

For years I've had insomnia, it's an integral part of me,
I begged to be referred but the Drs couldn't see,
Because I'd learned to function on so very little sleep,
They couldn't grasp the problem so I continued counting sheep.

20 years of asking and always being told no,
I had a new Consultant, thought I'd give it one more go,
In exasperation, I pleaded just one more time,
To acknowledge how this issue must affect this head of mine.

We filled out the referral but we didn't hold much hope,
There was help for sleep disorders, but insomnia…nope,
I was nowhere near the points that would say that I deserved,
But we sent it off anyway and prayed that I'd be heard.

The appointment made me anxious, but I can totally recall,
The reaction deep inside of me as I watched her write it all,
I looked at her confused as I could very clearly see,
I remember saying the words, "you actually believe me??"

She didn't know my history so she didn't understand,
How many interactions just didn't go as planned,
Accused of being an actress, attention was my aim,
But this Dr didn't doubt me, she didn't add more pain.

She's like no consultant I have ever met before,
I often hear her laughter before I walk through her door,
She doesn't realise that she's treating much more than my sleep,
She asks about my life and her compassion runs so deep.

With every interaction the respect she shows is true,
She thanks me for **my** time, her approach is something new,
She removes the power imbalance, we're an equal bodied team,
I trusted her from the start, she'll never know how much that means.

I don't know how long I'll have her and although I waited years,
I couldn't wish for a better Dr for my insomnia and my fears,
She showed me she's a person with a heart so big and true,
No pretence, she's authentic, and the beauty of that shines through.

Angela McCrimmon

2 Of Us On A Journey

For years she didn't see me, maybe didn't have the time,
The appointments are so quick, or I wasn't showing signs,
I only reached out when I was in deep distress,
She didn't see the contrast, that sometimes more is less.

It took everything I had to get through her office door,
Everything screamed "they can't help you anymore,"
I'd come out so defeated for albeit she was kind,
Someone higher up was pulling all the strings.

She'd been instructed how to treat me, "it's for her own good,"
Why were they not concerned about my suicidal mood?
I'm rarely suicidal so it wasn't a common thing,
My heart hit the floor, there was no point in anything.

There was a crucial turning point and the powers from above,
Removed her from my care or maybe she was shoved?
The huge difference in my treatment almost overnight,
Slowly, and together, we turned the wrong back into right.

We had follow up appointments, arranged them in advance,
I could avoid the reception and their own merry dance,
We monitored my mood to see how high or low,
And also the duration of stability I showed.

She learned my personality and what made up my world,
We laughed together openly on the days in which I whirled,
Into her office and spoke just like a train,
Then jumped out my chair and whirled back out again.

She's been on this journey with me and I have such respect,
She's taken time to learn and to always just reflect,
To know me well enough, to listen from the heart,
She sees me, not just my notes, and that's where they should start.

Person-Centred Care

Last year I got the chance to see care at its best,
An inpatient stay that stood out from the rest,
The compassion they showed for my sensitive state,
They knew when to push and they knew when to wait.

They were treating some burns but I wanted to stay,
At home if I could and return every day,
As the weeks went by the nurse could see,
The depression I felt was crippling me.

I'd underestimated the damage I'd done to myself,
The main problem though was my mental health,
I was on the verge where I just couldn't engage,
It wasn't their job, but my life they saved.

They all said that they'd never seen me so low,
I'll never forget the respect that they showed,
Encouraged to shower but when I'd sit up to try,
I'd stare at the bathroom for hours and just cry.

When they'd suggested admission I felt my heart break,
For I felt so much guilt, yet again I would take,
A bed in a unit that's so special and rare,
Self-Harm screams, "You don't deserve to be there!"

My depression worsened to such a degree,
I tried to strangle the life out of me,
Psych ward referral, they had every right,
But instead they sat with me all day and all night.

They've known me for quite a number of years,
They'd never seen me like this with so many tears,
They'd never seen me so broken where I'd lost all hope,
But their care and compassion truly helped me to cope.

"**Wallace Burns Unit**"……you deserve to be named,
Where so many times I have felt so ashamed,
You treated my wounds but not just those you could see,
In the way that you cared, you helped heal part of me.

The Body Remembers.....

I know she's never hurt me but somehow I still believe,
Psychiatry is a threat and somehow they do deceive,
The feeling that I get from my head down to my toes,
A fight or flight response and she doesn't even know.

Appointment date draws closer and I start to feel unwell,
A dread inside my stomach for a story I can't tell,
Sleepless nights precede and my anxiety runs high,
I panic when she calls me and I really don't know why.

It shows me that the trauma is really quite profound,
My body still responds to the memories and sound,
A history so hurtful, years of being dismissed,
Finally put on one... then taken off the waiting list!

She's never caused me damage, she turned it all around,
She found the missing piece when my world was upside down,
I hope that maybe somehow, with time my heart will heal,
And it's her care that I'll remember, not old trauma that I feel.

Complex Post Traumatic Stress Disorder

I see her every week , she was definitely worth the wait,
It's a 2 year waiting list for Psychology to date,
I feel like she "gets me" and I try hard to engage,
It's like sharing my book of life and working through each page.

She asks me a question and actually waits for my reply,
If I can't find the words she gently helps me try,
She'll come up with a hypothesis and ask if I resonate,
I'm free to tell her "nope," and we laugh at her mistake.

I'm used to a hypothesis or conclusion being found,
Appearing in my notes, being promptly written down,
To follow me through life yet not once did I agree,
They just ticked another box and medicalised me.

We've uncovered lots of trauma which I have always known,
I was turned away for years and left to cope alone,
It's left me in a space now when at times when she is kind,
I find it overwhelming and the pain is quite refined.

I asked the outright question, "Tell me what you see?"
She looked down at her notes then looked back up at me,
"I know you have Bipolar but I see Complex Trauma too,"
My heart stood still in shock for I guess I always knew.

I wished I hadn't asked but there was one more thing to say,
Inside my heart was breaking with acknowledgment that day,
"Can you fix me?" I asked, or has my fate been sealed?
"You're not broken" she replied, and one day this will be healed.

Angela McCrimmon

Diagnosis Drug Seeking

I could hear it immediately when I answered my phone,
That air of disgust mixed with boldness in his tone,
"So what do you want from me?" were his very straight words,
"I was hoping you could make this pain stop to hurt??"

I'd had an injury on my arm almost one year before,
It was worse than any harm I had ever done before,
No surgery required, must be a lucky situation,
In time I learned their only option would have been an amputation!

So the plan was my nurse would treat it 3 times a week,
I could barely let her touch me for the damage was so deep,
I asked her one day "what are those things that look like trees?"
"They're your nerves and your veins," Struck dumb in disbelief.

It doesn't take a genius to imagine the level of pain,
My Dr referred me to a Pain Specialist again,
For the dose she could prescribe just wasn't cutting through,
But we knew that they could help, if he'd only wanted to.

He went through what I'd tried with clear disdain on his tongue,
He told me each drug I'd tried, not missing any one,
I pointed out that there were some which I didn't even finish,
Never mind look for more, but his interest had diminished.

I tried to stay rational and think maybe I was wrong,
How can he think I'm "drug seeking" when the pain's gone on this long?
If he'd seen the damage done, he'd surely understand,
I was absolutely genuine but he held the upper hand.

He then began to recite my Psychiatric medication,
That's when I knew I could read the situation,
I was consulting him for pain so to do just what he'd done,
Was disrespectful and insulting to me and everyone.

Everyone else treating me, especially the one,
Who had made the referral to see what could be done,
I came off that call no better than I was before,
Diagnosis "Drug seeking" as he threw me out the door.

Treatment Room Nurse

She doesn't even realise how much she's helping me,
She's giving me some routine and for me that holds the key,
As I surfaced from depression, it got me out of bed,
I asked to go to her than have them come to me instead.

I'd met her once before but never around self-harm,
I was nervous of her judgment but she was gentle and so calm,
She didn't look shocked, no sense of her disgust,
I very quickly learned that this was someone I could trust.

3 times a week so we got to know each other well,
We'd exhausted all the small talk, so stories we would tell,
We loved all animals, adored dogs both big and small,
She still missed her "Pepsi," her most special dog of all.

She took care of my dressings but she gave me time to talk,
The value of that time and space could not be bought,
I'd share with her my plans, entertaining her with rhyme,
She'd check that I remembered to factor in "Me time."

We'd often laugh and joke and sometimes even say,
"If anyone could hear us they would carry us away!!"
But the beauty of those moments is I knew there was no mask,
She was genuine and authentic as she went about the task.

I have a long way to go but one day the wounds will heal,
My routine will change and the gap will feel quite real,
But with every interaction she's gently reminding me,
What the qualities and compassion of a good nurse should be.

Trauma -v- Depression

They tell me it's "trauma" but I'm begging them to see,
This "trauma" has triggered a depressive episode for me,
I know the difference for I've been here many times before,
I'm screaming out for help but there's no sound anymore.

I was going through the motions for it hadn't happened yet,
I wasn't quite depressed but I could feel the disconnect,
I woke up in the morning and somehow in a daze,
I went to bed at night and had made it through the day.

Then one day it was dark, my body felt so weak,
I lay in bed for weeks and could barely even speak,
The very thought of washing was enough to bring on tears,
I knew it had arrived, the depression of my fears.

Caring for myself was impossible for me,
But it broke my heart in 2 when I knew I couldn't be,
The carer and protector of my faithful fluffy friend,
My dog, my everything, to friends I had to send.

In hospital I must have cried at least a million tears,
2 months in this state, fulfilling all my fears,
For as long as they confused it with trauma I could see,
The help I knew I needed was being denied to me.

I couldn't see the light, I just couldn't carry on,
My life was in their hands and I knew they'd got it wrong,
I saw no other answer but to finally make it stop,
Unsuccessful… but what a soul wrenching guilt that it brought.

I don't know what changed but somehow in the end,
The depression was acknowledged and I was finally on the mend,
The medication I had asked for at least 2 months before,
I'd known what I needed but they thought they knew me more.

Each day I've grown stronger and I felt my smile return,
I regained my interest in the projects I'd begun,
I've put it in the past but it's left me with a deep fear,
Will they believe me the next time I say my depression is here?

A Broken System

I feel sad when I think about the damage they have done,
A system so broken, if a battle they'd have won,
I'd resigned myself to always being misunderstood,
They only saw my weaknesses and overlooked the good.

Going to the Emergency Room would fill me with such dread,
I needed their help, but I knew they'd hurt me instead,
With no time to spare a Doctor barely reviewed,
The last page of my notes and agreed they thought it too.

This wouldn't be a problem if my notes had been correct,
But they had a textbook version, it wasn't me they would reflect,
With each wrong assumption my heart would break some more,
It wasn't long until the pieces were all scattered on the floor.

They caused me so much trauma that never should have been,
I kept it locked inside too scared that I'd be seen,
As a "manipulative, attention seeking" person if I voiced,
So I stayed silent in fear, I didn't have much choice.

How on earth was I meant to trust, when each time we'd interact,
They couldn't see beyond the notes, couldn't see they weren't facts,
Some of the descriptions were a literal "copy and paste,"
From the diagnostic manual, they had no time to waste.

I'm in a very different place now with a very different team,
They recognise I'm "complex" and not always as I seem,
I'm not ungrateful for their care but I still regret the day,
I entered a system that would damage me this way.

Angela McCrimmon

Creative Communication

I woke up today with a feeling of dread,
A million thoughts raced through my head,
Should I go back to sleep or cancel the call?
Or maybe just not even attend it at all?

It's been in my diary, I had marked the date,
A step forward in an attempt to communicate,
I'd had an idea and they were willing to see,
If it could help other patients, just like me.

I smile when I think back to the day,
I sent my first "Newsletter" on its way,
Goodness knows what my Psychiatrist thought,
I was worried she'd think I had lost the plot!!

I just realised that sometimes the appointment time,
Was consumed with sharing this life of mine,
If I sent it before, we'd be one step ahead,
And she'd see the "bigger picture" instead.

I could show her my world in a way that reflects,
A true picture of me that my appointments neglect,
So much happens between seeing her last,
And our time to talk always goes by so fast!

So today we're having a video call,
But today I won't be her patient at all,
The imbalance of power for today is gone,
For I stand alongside which is where I belong.

Respect

I can still recall that very day,
As if it was only yesterday,
In the ward I lay in that hospital bed,
And I made a promise within my head.

I promised myself that if I survived,
If somehow I found myself still alive,
I'd find a way to raise my voice,
To be heard and finally given a choice.

I promised that I would find some way,
To fight for myself and others one day,
When I reflect upon the last few years,
My promise fulfilled and I faced my fears.

For all the years I felt their neglect,
I feel like I've finally earned their respect,
I'm so thankful that I pushed on through,
Even when I didn't know what to do.

Together we've been on a journey where,
They recognised where to alter my care,
Forever grateful they were willing to learn,
And because of that, my respect was earned.

Angela McCrimmon

When Your Past Comes Calling

You hear stories on television regarding Dr's who abuse,
You read it in the paper when some stories hit the news,
But you're never quite prepared when you turn the page to see,
"Patient A" in this case is referring straight to me!

I had finally spoken out after over 20 years,
So much had kept me silent, so much had fueled my fears,
Did I think that they'd believe me? Did my story seem absurd?
Absolutely yes, but they believed my every word.

As my eyes read the headlines I felt it deep inside,
"Thank goodness I'm anonymous," I still felt I should hide,
It shocked me to realise that I still hold so much shame,
Simply because I still feel completely half to blame.

As I read over details I tried to disconnect,
To accept this was my story, I just wasn't ready yet,
I imagined his family as they'd come to realise,
His adamance of innocence was nothing more than lies.

As the story concluded and the consequence was shared,
Erased from the Register, Struck off for being impaired,
I felt my heart respond in a way that made me feel,
"It's over now Angela… and it's time for you to heal."

Trauma Talking

I have to achieve highly or it's not worth taking part,
Maybe then she'll say "well done" and I'll feel it in my heart,
"I'm proud of you," but I know those words could never be,
It's just my "Trauma talking" speaking right back at me.

I'm comfortable 1-1 but put me in a larger group,
I'm overwhelmed and panicked, my brain's stuck in a loop,
I've tried for many years with this problem trying to face,
It's just my "trauma talking" keeping me in my place.

I trust the world in general but there is a very certain kind,
That twists up my emotions and messes with my mind,
The medical profession, I trust so very few,
It's just my "trauma talking"....maybe it's talking to you?

People speak of being lonely but I love to be alone,
I feel a peace inside whenever I'm at home,
No social anxieties to be triggered through my day,
It's just my "trauma talking" ...but what's it trying to say?

It's trying to say be gentle and see us as unique,
Different reactions and experience to speak,
We're fragile but we're stronger than you could ever know,
We've survived when we thought we had nowhere else to go.

It's just my "trauma talking" when I beg you to take care,
We're all still healing and for some we're not quite there,
With every interaction I'm pleading that you'll see,
I'm trying my very best and fighting to be free.

Everywhere I turn right now it's the "buzz phrase" that I hear,
Without "Trauma Informed Practice" the cost could be so dear,
Be aware of Complex Trauma, so you know if trauma's there,
Reflect upon your practice, "Is this trauma informed care??"

And so we are on this mission to help you understand,
How broad the spectrum is when trauma takes a stand,
It's messy and it's complex but all we ask for is respect,
And if our trauma starts to talk, gently help us reconnect.

Angela McCrimmon

A Plastic Surgeon With A Heart

For years I really struggled to look him in the eye,
So sure of his judgment which would always make me cry,
A Plastic Surgeon who had seen me time after time,
Each time I had damaged this body of mine.

I must have cost thousands with each operation,
Undoing his work must have caused such frustration,
But something changed and I'm not sure why,
The day I found the courage to meet his eye.

I saw his compassion and such a gentle soul,
He wasn't angry with me even slightly at all,
He cared that I had been in such emotional pain,
That had landed me back in his care once again.

He had words of encouragement when it had been a while,
Acknowledging my progress, he would make me smile,
Where once I was so sure he resented my harm,
It was clear he just wished he could bring me some calm.

Over the years I developed deep trust,
When trauma hit hard I insisted it must,
Be him that treated all the damage incurred,
He understood why I was so deeply disturbed.

I'll never forget how for so many years,
I'd bow my head in shame as I tasted my tears,
I hope I'll never again need his care,
But I'll always be grateful for the times he was there.

Oscar Winning Performance

Today I'm doing something I never thought I'd do,
I'll share with you my story if you'd allow me to,
For years I felt accused of being "over-dramatic,"
Suggesting my distress was an "attention-seeking" tactic!

There was dishonesty implied which really broke my heart,
Every word from my mouth was the truth on my part,
They decided I was "acting," no time for silly lies,
The damage they inflicted from all that they implied.

It left me with such terror, and I found I'd underplay,
I'd ask for help too late for fear of what they'd say,
My brain was fueled with fear and could only deal with fact,
It played out in my whole life, I'm a little sad for that.

Today is not a step, it's a massive giant leap,
To break through the barriers of the paranoia deep,
What other people think, I do not give a jot,
I know just what I am, and also what I'm not!

I'm going to "play" a patient, for new Drs coming through,
I've learned about my character and all her symptoms too,
The student has to ask vital questions to pass their exam,
To work out my diagnosis or at least a treatment plan.

The fact that I am "acting" about a health situation,
Is really nothing short of an amazing revelation,
So much trauma lives in here that I want to leave behind,
And the fun part of this Role Play is the condition **isn't** mine!

So for all the times they've told me my distress just isn't real,
If I'm really such the actress that they often made me feel,
Then today should be successful and I'll hold my head up high,
A huge source of trauma and I'm finally saying goodbye.

3
My Recipe for Wellbeing

" I won't let pain turn my heart into something ugly. I will show you that surviving can be beautiful….." Chrissy Ann Martine

We all have to walk our own paths and set out on our own journey but if there's one thing I've learned over the years it's that I have to be responsible for every step that I take. During a particularly hard time some words came into my mind and hit me like a thunderbolt. At the risk of sounding harsh they were simply, "Get up….Nobody is coming to save you!" I realised that day that while the Health Professionals could support me to find a baseline for stability, it was up to me to find out all the other things that would help me to remain as well as possible. It took digging down deep to find motivation that wasn't always there but thankfully a determination to create a life worth living was at the core of my being. It meant that I tried a multitude of more holistic things to help me alongside the medication and the ones I found helped me most remain a permanent part of my Emotional Tool Kit to this day. I would encourage everyone to remember that this is your one and only life and it's up to us to play an active role alongside the Health Professionals to discover what helps to bring out the best in us. For me personally, I have found exercise and diet to be a huge factor, journaling my thoughts and emotions out onto paper every day, losing myself in various kinds of Art and Music, maintaining a good sleep routine, surrounding myself with the right friends who revive my energy and don't just drain it, yoga to help soothe my nervous system and most importantly remembering that Self-Care isn't selfish, it's essential. I wouldn't let my phone run out of battery without charging it up fully so I apply the same importance to my wellbeing. If there is anything you take from this book then I hope that it will be the importance of being a Co-Pilot in your care, not a passive passenger. I might not know where I'm going yet but it doesn't mean I'm lost, and I certainly intend to enjoy the scenery along the way.

Head -V- Heart

"You always seem so happy"......I often hear that said,
The secret my dear friend is I live outside my head,
To realise there's a force more powerful than thought,
It shows me who I am....and also who I'm not.

My mind does a "risk assessment" everywhere I go,
It plants the seed of doubt for all I might not know,
It weighs up situations, adds on another pound,
It's chatter unremitting when there's no-one else around.

My head thinks it's conclusive and always in control,
It doesn't celebrate achievement, always setting goals,
Occasionally in protest my own sanity will leave,
"I think my brain's unwell"...or am I being deceived?

What if it's my heart that's trying hard to scream?
The feeling in my gut that knows just what I mean,
The silence in my soul that wants to say "I'm here,"
The emotions I was taught by psychiatry to fear.

What if it's my heart that my head has overtaken,
The child in my spirit that has truly been forsaken,
The cry of my conscience knowing its own truth,
What if these are things that have all been overlooked?

I find happiness in simple things that others cannot see,
I found that being authentic is the only way to be,
I learned if I'm not feeling good the first place I should start,
Is to simply ask the question...."What if it's my heart?"

Stage Fright

A life spent "Performing," played out upon a stage,
A script left unwritten, just lyrics on a page,
Going through the motions, take another bow,
Such a different world to the one I'm in right now.

Audience approval, trying so hard to please,
Now I please myself and feel much more at ease,
I learned that when my confidence was fueled from the outside,
My insecurities were triggered and I always had to hide.

Always on the move, my feet rarely touched the ground,
I told myself I'm happiest when there's no-one else around,
I value my solitude, but it came at such a cost,
Never in the photos, relationships were lost.

I lived on "Auto-Pilot," I often flicked a switch,
I somehow came to life, so smoothly, not a glitch,
My tears could turn to laughter but standing in the wings,
Was a longing to be me...not just "that girl who sings."

It took my world to crash, a volcano to explode,
I never could imagine how my life could just implode,
I lost my identity and it took some time to find,
Who I really was beyond the madness of my mind.

People just assume that I must surely grieve,
For the life that I lost, the career I had to leave,
For everything I was, the ambition put to rest,
I find I have acceptance and that sometimes more is less.

I'm grateful for the memories but I'm happy where I am,
I never give up hope and I do the best I can,
I learned that being authentic would lead me to be free,
There's no "performance" required when I'm simply being "Me."

Miracle Morning

My day begins early and the chance I do take,
For that very special time before the world wakes,
That time when it feels like just the world and me,
Are deciding together how my day shall be.

Do I jump out of bed or go back to sleep?
My to-do list foregone or the plans I will keep?
I'll get up and get my exercise out of the way,
Energy high for the rest of the day.

I write in my journals, not one but three,
They are each and all a reflection of me,
As I transfer all the thoughts in my head,
I make sense of them all on paper instead.

Shower time - how I love the smell,
The uplifting scent of my shower gel,
As I feel the water upon my face,
I prepare for the day and I'm ready to race.

My dog awakens to tell me it's time,
He'd like to be part of this world of mine,
Together we enjoy a beautiful walk,
Time with each other and time to talk.

Breakfast time, my favourite part,
I try to eat for a healthy heart,
"You are what you eat," they often say,
What I eat tends to depict my day.

I'm so grateful for this special time,
To align my thoughts with this heart of mine,
To prepare myself for the rest of the day,
"World...I'm ready....and I'm on my way!"

<u>Sing</u>

Some people live their lives just waiting for the light,
That moment when things fall into place,
I have to admit this has never been my plight,
I just don't have the patience or the space.

I hear excuses why the time might not be right,
And sometimes it just doesn't make much sense,
For others it's almost as if they even might,
Be terrified of potential consequence.

My own character has such "get up and go,"
It's easy to feel such frustration,
When people complain and inside I know,
They're the reason for their own causation.

Life won't change unless we change first,
It's a definite domino effect,
At the well of life you must feel the thirst,
Be damn sure that it's not over yet!

Life is so short and we don't know how long,
But I long for you to hear my plea,
Take chances, don't wait 'til they're singing your song,
Sing your own, even if you're off-key!

My Tribe

Never underestimate the value of your "Tribe,"
Don't settle for just "company" to walk right by your side,
Seek out those people, the ones you see reflect,
Your own beliefs and values, the ones in whom you "get."

I have lots of friends but my "Tribe" are just a few,
They're crucial to my wellbeing in everything I do,
In them I see a reflection of my very own soul,
Where I feel incomplete, they help to make me whole.

"Soul-Sisters," "Twin Flames"......cut from the same cloth,
These friendships are serendipitous and cannot be bought,
The friends you're in synch with to so such a great degree,
When I'm falling behind, my tribe walk back to help me.

We laugh and we giggle and we make no sense,
The protection we feel can be quite immense,
I'm loyal and I'm loving, and I will always try,
To be the friend you need , no questions why.

We look out for each other and will understand,
If tiredness makes us abandon our plans,
We take care of our "Tribe," so we tell you to rest,
"Self-Care" is essential and always the best.

I don't need excuses or feel the need to explain,
I'm accepted, I'm loved, and in return do the same,
For good mental health it's essential that you find,
Th "Tribe" that will help and encourage your mind.

Whiteboard's Aren't Just For Classrooms

I've learned in my life I need to be 1 step ahead,
To have a plan prepared for when I get out of bed,
Ok, a giant "whiteboard" may be seem a bit extreme,
But following it to the letter, my life runs like a dream.

I've never been a "lists" gal.....but my head has overload,
I was forgetting everything, not safe to cross the road,
I start with a diary, I like to see it written down,
Then I transfer it to a "planner" when there's no-one else around.

It's like I've written the script for my very own play,
It honestly helps to keeps my anxiety at bay,
Being able to read what I'm meant to do,
Leaves space in my brain for others things too.

I don't cope well when routines will change,
It used to upset me and I'd think I was strange,
We're all a bit different and the main thing I see,
Is how much it helps - my whiteboard and me.

There isn't a feeling at the end of the day,
For "Completed tasks" and I *wipe* them away,
The satisfaction I feel so deep in my soul,
As I begin to write out tomorrow's goals.

Panic Stations……5,4,3,3,1

Panic and anxiety are scary at their best,
I was proposed a "grounding technique" so put it to the test,
The concept around it was "5…4..3..2…1,"
To keep you in the moment, not allow your thoughts to run.

What are 5 things I can see? I looked around the room,
My windows, photographs, flowers in early bloom,
I also see a picture that means so much to me,
And motivational quotes, encouraging me to be.

What 4 things can I touch? I was sitting at my desk,
The most obvious to me was my laptop I guess,
I picked up a pen and rolled it between my hands,
A book, then my dog because he always understands.

Are there 3 things I can hear? This was out my comfort zone,
I just don't pay attention when I'm living on my own,
But I could hear the washing machine, spinning like a race,
I could hear my music playing and my printer keeping pace.

2 things I can smell, now this one should be good,
I surround myself with scents to help impact my mood.
I could smell many things but to narrow it to 2,
My essential oil vaporiser and my own perfume too.

The last mindful practice of this amazing technique,
Is "name one thing I can taste," I can answer as a speak,
I can taste my toothpaste, so minty, fresh and clean,
According to the box, in 2 weeks my teeth will gleam.

This is something I'd heard of but I'd never given time,
So sure this was too simple for this complex head of mine,
But when I find myself accelerating to a place I can't be found,
I try 5,4,3,2,1 and I land safely on the ground.

Befriending

They asked the question...."What does befriending mean to me?"
With a moment of reflection it was clear for me to see,
Befriending fills my heart with a little ray of sun,
Just knowing I'm making a difference to the life of someone.

There was a time in life when a Befriender came to me,
I wasn't coping well and they helped me just to see,
That I could open up and talk, together we had fun,
I felt a little sad when the session would be done.

When our time together finished for the very last time,
I'd made a little promise within this heart of mine,
That one day I'd give back to a service so deserving,
I would take part in life instead of just observing.

Befriending gives me purpose and I love to see them smile,
To give them a chance to laugh, if only for a while,
To forget that life is hard, just one step at a time,
To ease their isolation, no mountain they can't climb.

I look forward to befriending no matter what their age,
I read their book of life and together we turn the page,
When I needed a befriender, she made me feel worthwhile,
I'll never forget that she reminded me how to smile.

So to answer the question, "what does befriending mean to me?"
There are so many reasons and it's a privilege to be,
A part of someone's life that years down the line,
They'll remember with a smile, a smile that matches mine.

See Me Scotland
(Scotland's Anti-Stigma Organisation)

There are a few organisations where it's an exciting place to be,
But none more exciting than one in Scotland called "See Me,"
They fight discrimination and stigma to the core,
I volunteer my time for them, yet I get so much more.

They value "lived experience" and always offer choice,
Over the last few years they have helped me find my voice,
Well ok, I had the voice but the platform they provide,
Is one which is respected and reaches Nationwide.

I never know what opportunity that they might throw my way,
There's never any pressure and sometimes I'll even say,
"Sorry, I'm just not feeling good, my energy is low,"
To know that I can say that, with no guilt is how I know.

I'm with the right people as I help out with campaigns,
I'm more than a "patient," I'm must more than just a "name,"
They're full of encouragement when I have moments of self-doubt,
They remind me that this "cause" is what I am all about!

To help create a world where we can live stigma-free,
Mental health won't be "hushed" and will be spoken of freely,
Barriers broken as this movement sweeps on through,
It's a privilege to be a part of such an amazing thing to do.

They've played quite a big part in where I stand today,
They've given me a voice and it's done in such a way,
That the platform they give me already holds such respect,
So the voice of lived experience we find is always met....

...Met with real interest, we are valued so much more,
I can remember in the past when people would have closed the door,
But thanks to their campaigning it's becoming clear to me,
The voice of lived experience really does hold the key.

We need the Professionals, of course they have their place,
But slowly I think even they are beginning to make space,
To see that we are people, lives beyond our mental health,
Understanding our experience has a currency of wealth.

So thank you to "See Me" for everything you do,
To fight discrimination and for all the groundwork too,
The campaigns that I've been part of all help my self-esteem,
Thanks to you I'm not afraid for my mental health to be seen.

On A Mission To Sleep

We're told about "Sleep Hygiene" when we say we cannot sleep,
We're handed sheets of paper for us to read and keep,
I'd tried all the usual things 20,000 times,
And then one day I created a "sleep hygiene" of mine.

My day starts at 3am so I need to compromise,
By starting bedtime early, preparing to close my eyes,
I soak in the bath in pure essential oils,
A mixture intended for sleep, insomnia I'll foil.

I have blackout curtains hanging in my room,
To block out any sunlight and to bring the darkness soon,
I have a Salt Lamp by my bed that gives a gentle glow,
I try to put into practice everything I know.

I use essential oils in my room diffuser too,
Every day I'm learning what each one can do,
For bedtime I always choose a nice relaxing blend,
I love the scent it gives and the message that it sends.

My "weighted blanket" will now come into play,
It was something I'd bought in desperation one day,
It goes over my duvet but doesn't make me hot,
But the blanket adds 9kg of weight on top!

I wasn't convinced it would have an effect,
But I wasn't prepared to give up just yet,
The weight of the blanket was steady and strong,
And it keeps me settled all night long!

Next is my eye mask with speakers for ears,
Sleeping in silence just fills me with fear,
So I link an audiobook to play from my phone,
And it plays though my mask so I'm never alone.

My final piece of the puzzle is a secret device,
It sounds a bit crazy and you'll maybe think twice,
From my hand a tiny microcurrent will sweep,
Sends a message to my brain to tell it to sleep!

Medication is needed just to get me to sleep,
But these secrets I've shared are what truly keep,
My mind at peace for each long night,
My own "Sleep Hygiene" keeps everything right.

Voice of Reason

I can't sit back if I see injustice done,
My life would be much easier if I could!
Where others will turn their backs and run,
I stand strong if my heart tells me I should.

It's not that I'm being "nosy" or "busying" around,
Your own privacy is surely yours to hold,
But if I see you mistreated, I may not make a sound,
But I'll ensure the right sources will be told.

I'm not a superhero nor do I want to be,
I'm just someone who always needs to know,
That if the person in need of some help was me,
Someone would step forward and show.

The world is conditioning us to make no fuss,
Believe me when I say that this is true,
I believe in the power of praise just as much,
And will give credit wherever credit is due.

Don't stand on the side lines when there's cruelty around,
Take courage and believe in what you do,
Your giving someone a voice who can't yet make a sound,
For just one moment let them speak through you.

January Blues

I hear people complaining of the "January Blues,"
They say this is the month they always dread,
I guess I just don't "get" it as to me I always choose,
To feel such gratitude and excitement instead.

I think I must be lucky for I often hear them say,
How the weather and the cold just get them down,
Whether sunshine or rain I appreciate the day,
And find pleasure in the beauty all around.

I have food in my tummy and a warm bed at night,
I have clothes to wear, shoes upon my feet,
I can warm up my home and I have electric light,
Some people are surviving on the streets.

I have people who love me and whom I love in return,
A little doggy who's been sent from up above,
It shouldn't make a difference whether rain or sun,
The secret is to fill your heart with love.

Love the sound of laughter, find healing in your tears,
Treasure all the memories you make,
Take care of your body as we all advance in years,
Delight in opportunities you take.

If you struggle in January please know I sympathise,
Just try to keep perspective in your mind,
Each month and every season comes with lows and highs,
If we look hard enough it's beauty that we'll find.

Angela McCrimmon

Special Occasions

I was raised to take care of gifts I'd been bought,
On "Special Occasions" they'd appear,
Then I'd carefully put it back in the box,
And bring it back out for next year.

I'd watch my mother do the very same thing,
So her behaviour I'd replicate,
As another box of chocolates home she would bring,
Untouched until they were out of date!

As the years passed by and my health would fail,
I discovered the beauty that lay,
In realising the "Special occasion" we fail,
To see is right here... today!!!

I now use all the things I couldn't afford,
Bathe in all the best creams,
All the "special" things I'd have usually stored,
Become part of my daily regime.

At night when I am getting ready for bed,
I love the room to smell nice,
Sometimes I'll spray my best perfume instead,
After all, you don't live twice.

So cherish today and realise the treasure,
Is simply being here and alive,
This "special occasion" can never be measured,
I just celebrate the fact I survived!

Pay it Forward

Today is a special day that I never thought would come,
It's been a very long process, and it wasn't an easy one,
It's a day of excitement, of trepidation and of fear,
But it's been well worth the wait and the day is finally here.

If I mentioned the 5 July, back in 1948,
Would it mean anything, or just a random date?
This date makes me emotional for I know that it's true,
It was the start of something special for me and for you.

On this day our National Health Service came to be,
If Healthcare was needed we could access it free,
What a gift and privilege that if we needed Healthcare,
No pennies to rub, but it would always take good care.

As I entered the world almost 30 years later,
By my choice I would rather have been a spectator,
But reality chose that this wasn't to be,
"Well acquainted" are the NHS and me.

So today is the day I will give up some time,
Volunteering a few hours from this life of mine,
Without the NHS I'd don't know where I'd be,
I'll be the proudest volunteer you ever will see.

Angela McCrimmon

Authenticity

I stumbled upon a lesson that's now the essence of me,
I learned the huge importance of authenticity,
I don't mean I was dishonest, but so much I tried to hide,
My own opinions, thoughts, and feelings were stuffed back down inside.

I held so many secrets that I felt I'd never tell,
I'd look you in the eye and tell you that I'm well,
When in reality I was almost down upon my knees,
Living in fight or flight and in the latter stages, freeze.

I was scared of speaking up for always being shut down,
I was terrified of treatment with no-one else around,
So for all I longed to tell you how much that you were wrong,
I bowed my head in shame thinking that's where I belonged.

I felt a change inside of me and I'm really not sure why,
I knew I had to live my truth or I would surely die,
I had to be authentic for my heart to be at peace,
It's been the key to my freedom and I felt my mind release.

If someone asks a question I now answer from my heart,
My mind will overthink so I stop it before it starts,
I do what makes me happy, I fill up my own soul,
I learned that being authentic would help me become whole.

Authenticity is a precious thing because it means I'm being real,
I no longer apologise for explaining how I feel,
Each day I am learning so many different ways to be,
The most genuine and authentic version of me.

Stolen Moments

I awaken in the morning and the first thing that I do,
Is throw wide my curtains, say "God, I'm thanking you,"
For another day to live and to show how much I care,
I open up my window, breathe in the fresh morning air.

The world is very silent when it's only 3 o'clock,
I feel I'm stealing moments that others have forgot,
Like the sound of the birds singing in such beautiful bird song,
It keeps me being mindful and this reminder is so strong.

I get to work on projects, it feels so pressure free,
For the world is still asleep and not expecting much from me,
I write in all my journals, I catch-up with email,
I'll maybe write a poem, give amazon a sale.

I'll squeeze into my gym clothes, a workout in itself,
I know it's so important to help my mental health,
To get all the endorphins racing through my blood,
With all these happy chemicals, my body soon will flood.

I start my day off slowly and it helps me feel prepared,
I know what's going to happen and I don't feel just as scared,
I might have a busy day but I break it into parts,
No overwhelming feelings, not knowing where to start.

As I write I can feel the cool morning air on my skin,
The birds are singing softly, my day shall now begin,
With gratitude I thank the world for my place,
I want us all to win, for this life is not a race.

New Year Resolutions

New year resolutions, people making plans,
They ask me what mine are but they wouldn't understand,
Looking to the future is such a luxury to me,
I take one day at a time and that's how it has to be.

Of course I have ambitions, I have my hopes and dreams,
But when you have a mental illness they often go downstream,
However, like a river there are twists and there are turns,
The water keeps on running and I'll feel my strength return.

I'm not looking for your pity and I don't pin any blame,
My life's not what I expected but I'm happy all the same,
I find pleasure in such simple things that others might not see,
Gratitude is essential and I'm thankful to be me.

I don't plan lavish holidays for I cannot guarantee,
That when they come around I'll be ready and carefree,
Many trips have been abandoned and flights I've let slip by,
It was a very expensive lesson that my money had to buy.

So what are my resolutions for the year 2022?
To be more present in the moment making memories with you,
To find balance in myself, in my world and in my day,
To pause before jumping into things that come my way.

I resolve to take good care of every part of me,
To show myself more kindness, reminding me to be,
Patient with myself and self-forgiving too,
I resolve to love myself in 2022.

«Trouble»

"Trouble" is my 4-legged furry friend,
Much more than "just a dog" could ever be,
He's such a gift from God that only He could send,
To make up the most amazing part of me.

He's there in the morning when I open my eyes,
Snuggled tight, curled up in a heap,
You'd think he would sense I was starting to rise,
But one look says, "I'm trying to sleep!!"

So I get myself ready and leave him in peace,
To wake up in his own doggy time,
Singing out loud, I'm the radio police,
He gives in and the doggy is mine!

There's no denying he has a heart of gold,
On our walks he just bounces along,
Saying hello to both young and old,
He senses if something is wrong.

He picks up on feelings, senses a vibe,
To draw closer or give them some space,
He senses those people to just walk beside,
And which others to lick in the face!

He loves to go traveling, 'adventure.com,'
Traveling companions together,
My best buddy, I talk to him all day long,
Brings me sunshine no matter the weather.

His little character makes me laugh out loud,
His human traits are very amusing,
Without a doubt he stands out in a crowd,
And he adores a "treat" to be chewing.

My best friend, Trouble is so precious I say,
Through this life we have traveled together,
Helping my mental health every day,
He's an antidepressant I'd take forever!

Angela McCrimmon

Granny Joyce and Trouble

Happy at Doggy Daycare

Bedtime cuddles with Teddy

The Rules

My Heart

I focus on the brain so much as that's where it all goes on,
A realisation hit me, there's another part so strong,
A part we take for granted so with great gratitude I'll start,
Acknowledging the strength of my whole amazing heart.

Put aside the physical for we know it pumps our blood,
But who's the one with open arms when our emotions start to flood?
When tears are falling endlessly and I'm sure I'll fall apart,
The place holding and reassuring me is my dear forgotten heart.

It's there in times of laughter or with pride I feel it swell,
It holds a million memories of stories it could tell,
It's there in times of tragedy, absorbing all the pain,
But with overwhelming strength, it fills back up again.

It tells me what's important because I'll feel a disconnect,
It talks to me and answers, even if it is "not yet,"
It's with me as I fall in love on that rollercoaster ride,
It's kept beating through each heartbreak and been right by my side.

I can't think of a stronger part of me that fuels my fire inside,
When I'm close to giving up, it's the thing that turns the tide,
It's shattered in a million pieces, jagged parts upon the floor,
It tells me what's worth fighting for and when to close the door.

So today I'm saying thank you to this amazing part of me,
It's my heart, not my mind that needs to feel set free,
I've learned that if my heart's content, I can feel it still my mind,
My heart holds so much hope that my brain can't always find.

4
Life In Lockdown

"In the rush to return to normal, use the time to consider which parts of "normal" are worth rushing back to – Dave Hollis

On 23 March 2020, the Prime Minister of our time , Boris Johnston declared that the United Kingdom was officially in lockdown due to the alarmingly contagious spread of a Virus we all came to know as Covid-19. The Virus started in China and spread worldwide at a deadly rate, reaching the UK with its first confirmed case on 29 January 2020. The world came to a standstill and we were only allowed to leave the house for medical needs, food, or to care for a vulnerable person. Social Distancing was brought in where people had to be 2 metres apart from each other and for a very long time you could only meet with one person at a time. This Global Pandemic devastated lives and many of us feared the end of the world was in sight. To date, in June 2022 there have been 536.63 million people infected globally and 6,977,728 deaths. The world changed as we know it and people were having to lose loved ones without being able to say goodbye because of restrictions to stay at home. Funerals were even live-streamed online to avoid large group gatherings. It was a tragic time and scientific research teams were racing against the clock to try and find a vaccine to combat this virus that was rapidly wiping out the population. How proud should we feel that on 8 December, 2020, the UK became the first country in the world to deliver an approved COVID-19 Vaccine. Some people were and are still very resistant to accepting the vaccine but personally, I welcomed it and was glad that most of the people I know and love also did. However, I respect everyone has a choice and I just pray that if any of those unvaccinated do catch Covid then their symptoms won't be too severe. As I write, most of the restrictions have been lifted, the world is resuming to a semi somewhat 'normal' state and organisations seem to be delivering services half in person and half via the internet - technically known as "hybrid."

I wanted to acknowledge that I am aware of just what a tragic and terrible time people have had and for people with mental health conditions we all responded in different ways. Most people I know hated the isolation and suffered from extreme loneliness but because social anxiety plays a major part in my life, the day we went into lockdown there was a huge part of me that could not have felt more relieved. Not just for the sake of my physical safety but more so for all the anxiety that being part of the world "in person" creates for me.....it's like someone just pushed a button and I came down from high alert and settled into a much more settled state of being. It's like I then created a world within the world and this new world I had created worked for me! I stayed very much engaged with the world online, joining the rest of the population as we got to grips with Video Calls....does "You're on mute!!" sound familiar?? However, the anxiety I feel when I engage with people in person was lifted from my shoulders and if anything I am still trying to adjust to coming out of lockdown, which happened on 19 July 2021. I actually cried for a full week and had to keep the News turned off for the weeks before it as we continually heard about this forthcoming lifting of restrictions. I knew that I would have to learn to re-engage with the world in person again which would mean feeling the unbearable embodiment of anxiety while trying to appear like a perfectly functioning adult who was taking it all in her stride. In the first few weeks when we came out of lockdown, the only strides I made were back to my bed in tears. I felt like I had been climbing a mountain for years, constantly trying to acclimatise myself to interacting with people without it leaving me utterly drained and exhausted because I had so much adrenaline racing around my body - invisible of course - and suddenly I was back at the bottom of the mountain and the mountain had grown even bigger than before.

As you read what my personal experience of lockdown was I felt like it was important that I make it clear that I'm aware it had some devastating impacts of so many lives, I just happen to be someone that found out life in lockdown was easier than reality for me. My heart goes out to those who lost loved ones or for those still suffering with mental health problems that increased or even surfaced for the very first time during this surreal time we have all been part of.

Lockdown Week 1

I woke up today with a feeling of dread,
Do I even get up or get out of bed?
With nowhere to go and nothing to do,
Makes me feel sick… how about you?

LOCKDOWN… We all knew it must come,
Photos of Brits all packed in the sun,
"Social distancing" far from their mind,
Taking a risk of wiping out mankind.

Some of us will spend this time all alone,
Our lifeline becoming the telephone,
No contact with family or even a friend,
"Not essential? Don't go!" is the message it sends.

Keep in perspective what's really going on,
This lockdown really won't be for too long,
We're not going to war, being sent out to die,
We've to stay in and be safe to keep us alive!

Pray for the "keyworkers" who've been given no choice,
If you won't listen to Government then please hear their voice,
At risk and in tears, they are down on their knees,
"Please stay at home," is the message they plead.

In a world so uncertain of course we are scared,
Never been here before so all unprepared,
Employment and incomes are all put on hold,
We need the Government's voice to be clear and be bold.

Our moods will be tested, emotions run high,
Kids drive you crazy as you break down and cry,
Our worlds transfer to meetings online,
Adapt with this world and just give it time.

Day one of lockdown and I'm feeling quite sane,
A few weeks from now we know that could change,
Be safe my friends and at the end of each day,
Be thankful and always remember to pray.

Lockdown Week 2

The world as we know it has all been torn away,
The things I do to keep me well to navigate each day,
The routine that I follow to keep me on the ground,
It's scary as I realise that my world is upside down.

I tell myself "don't panic!" as anxieties run high,
Radical acceptance and no longer asking why,
"Self-Isolation" is the phrase I often hear,
I pick up the telephone to keep my loved ones near,

I take my medication in the morning when I wake,
Reminding me the value of the effort I must make,
My mental health could suffer if I don't stay self-aware,
It's vital that I always make the time for my self-care.

I'm learning every day that my routine is the key,
I need to find a purpose for the person I can be,
Exploring a new world that is flourishing online,
Repeating in my head that it's going to be just fine.

I don't need to feel lonely even though I am alone,
Video Chat, Facebook Friends that live inside my phone,
We're all in this together and we're going to see it through,
Emerging even stronger if it's the only thing we do!

I'll use this time to write, to exercise and cook,
I'll search inside my soul whilst devouring a book,
For once I will be still, not rushing here or there,
I'll help the vulnerable and always show I care.

My life is very different but different isn't bad,
Learning to let go of preconceptions that I had,
Holding onto sanity and working hard to find,
Peace within my soul, my body and my mind.

Eternal Gratitude

They step into the world not knowing what lies ahead,
Statistics rise, reality strikes, their hearts are full of dread,
"Protective Equipment? ...which department may I ask?
We're dealing with open wounds and yet we seem the last!"

The Nurses come to work, some heads are hanging low,
Sadness and loneliness because answers they don't know,
They're each a special angel, watching over everyone,
Long hours, constant care, whilst initiating fun.

No visitors allowed to brighten a patients day,
Carers are inventive, they're on their hands to play,
They won't let this loneliness make them down or sad,
Residents watch in awe, like the Nursing Home's gone mad!

"Why don't we build a jigsaw of old Edinburgh town?"
Smiles start to gather and they start to settle down,
"For those a bit more agile we can take a gentle stroll,
Albeit we're confined, maybe a game of indoor bowls?"

NHS, Healthcare and each Keyworker too,
Coming together to help us all get through,
You're part of history, you've nursed through Covid-19,
You put your own life at risk so your patients could be seen.

"Thank you" doesn't seem enough for everything you do,
Every day you're put at risk, and all your loved ones too,
I pray when this is over, your respect will reach the moon,
Thanks to all your efforts, the pandemic will be over soon.

Angela McCrimmon

Week 4 In Lockdown

Week 4 in Lockdown – the most challenging yet,
I heard myself scream, "Is it not over yet???"
I haven't a clue where my time was spent,
But my 'get up and go' just got up and went!

So many plans that I didn't fulfill,
Procrastination my greatest skill,
The "to do" list I wrote remains undone,
I avoided the world and everyone!

Anxiety hit hard with no reason why,
Distraction techniques I just couldn't try,
Irrational thoughts, frozen in fear,
Learning that this could go on all year.

Determined I must not lose my mind,
I got myself a "Therapist" online,
Video chat, just checking in,
Journal exploring my feelings within.

I'm usually quite happy being alone,
But it's just not the same on the telephone,
Family far and friends out of reach,
Lockdown providing some lessons to teach.

A new week ahead so I'm turning the page,
Signed up for lots and I plan to engage,
I'm feeling better as we enter week five,
I may be "locked down" but thank God I'm alive!

Lockdown Lessons

Life in lockdown isn't hard to see,
Tragic for some but a blessing for me,
Things that I have learned whilst being all alone,
Lessons I will treasure and seeds that have been sown.

I didn't grieve for the life that had but gone,
There was nothing to gain from seeing all the wrong,
We're living in a world with quite ludicrous rules,
Parents terrified to send their children to school.

I don't feel like I've faced lockdown alone,
As most of my friends reached out with their phone,
A little text here, a video call there,
I even came online without combing my hair!

I used journals to help me process my thoughts,
They really did open my eyes …a lot,
They helped me to see where a wound hasn't healed,
And gave me the tools to change how I feel.

Lockdown made me re-evaluate friends,
With a heavy heart I knew some would end,
I realised with some there was only "history" to see,
There's was nothing here and now that linked them to me.

Covid- 19 is such a tragic disease,
I watched on TV as the Nurses would plead,
The world was in chaos but I had an inner calm,
I think Lockdown reminded me just who I am.

Angela McCrimmon

Online Therapy

Lockdown hit when it hadn't been long,
Since I'd been admitted to a hospital ward,
I'd fallen to pieces, stopped singing my song,
And I knew it was the only way forward.

After 3 or 4 weeks I was ready to face,
The world, take a deep breath and fly,
A few weeks out and we heard of a case,
Of Co-vid, and that people might die.

People talked about how the isolation,
Would drive people to such despair,
Panic because there were no vacations,
"Unprecedented times" to be fair.

The memory of my recent hospital stay,
Was still very fresh in my mind,
I'd do anything to help me stay far away,
So I found a "therapist online."

I was sceptical at first because I'm not naive,
She'd have her work cut out with me,
I'm not someone who'll just accept and believe,
I need proof, I need something to see.

I filled in the forms explaining why,
I felt they could help me through,
I just wanted consistent input to try,
To maintain my "stability" too.

We hit it off from that very first day,
She brought comfort and challenge to me,
She provides a safe space where I'm open to say,
And she provides other perspectives to see.

She's from across the pond but with my laptop it seems,
That she's barely in a room down the hall,
Once a week for my "wellbeing routine,"
She helps catch me if I'm headed to fall.

Who knows how long I'll continue to use,
A therapist that I found online,
I had everything to gain and nothing to lose,
To hold onto this sanity of mine!

Please Remember...

The world has more awareness of people's mental health,
I've even heard some say that "their health is their wealth,"
The last 2 years have given them just a glimpse to see,
What some people live with.....and some permanently.

People had a taste of anxiety and depression for a while,
But when life resumed to "normal" they soon found their style,
For some of us it's still literally, one day at a time,
Not knowing until it gets here if we will be just fine.

The stigma still surrounding long term mental health,
If that could all be gone, therein for US lies the wealth,
Remember as the world returns, some still struggle through,
Our illness isn't temporary, more layers have been added too.

I haven't lost my hope that with a little gentle education,
You'd see the person, not the illness, and we'd feel no segregation.

Expectations -v- Reality

People lower their tone to ask me how I am,
"Are you coping with this dreaded lockdown?"
First of all I assure them that they absolutely can,
Turn up the volume and the sound.

When you have a mental illness people assume,
That it won't take much to push me over,
The irony being if there were many in the room,
I'd probably be the last one to fall over.

I hear of isolation and maybe I'm just strange,
But I haven't felt any loneliness at all,
I listen to my friends, some feel quite deranged,
I feel compassion and I feel their brick wall.

I think the key for me is I realised early days,
That the only way that I would survive,
Was to create some routine in so many ways,
It was different, but I continued to thrive.

I hear "I'm so bored" and I'm baffled by this,
There aren't enough hours in the day,
Of course there are things of "normality" I miss,
But there's still lots to do and to say.

My secret is simple, I go to bed each night,
With a structure and plan for tomorrow,
Covid threw our routines way out of sight,
So I just created a new one to follow.

Such Beauty Overlooked

We've heard for many years we need to get out and "connect,"
With the world of nature, it can help us to forget,
So good for mental health, such tranquillity to find,
But the truth is it bored me and my overactive mind.

I was always racing out the door, often running late,
What day is it today? Have I forgotten the actual date?
Up to my eyes in tasks with barely time to stop,
Eventually I'll remember whatever I've forgot.

I do respect nature, I just never take the time,
Then entered Lockdown and the rules were realigned,
Suddenly I was forced to take a daily walk,
More than one in fact, if only my dog could only talk.

From simply slowing down it opened up my soul,
The thing I had been missing now making me feel whole,
Fresh air in my lungs, listening to birds sing,
So beautiful as I wonder what the message is they bring,

I found myself by water to simply still my mind,
The ripples and the waves reflected this in time,
I can't wait for it to warm, for on the beach I'll roll,
Fueled with endorphins, Cold Water Swimming is my goal.

Without this lockdown I would still be in the dark,
Passing nature by, not making time for that,
But I can honestly say I feel gratitude and respect,
It's introduced me to nature and I will not forget.

Lockdown has given me a brand new routine,
Walking with friends, we all take in the scenes,
I'm rising up early to capture the sunrise,
Lockdown has certainly opened up my eyes.

So thank you lockdown for helping me to see,
All that I was missing that could be helping me,
I underrated nature, too busy in my mind,
From now on when it comes to nature....I'll always make the time!

Confused.Com

Oh my goodness, where do I start?
The world's gone mad, it's falling apart,
I'm so confused and I still don't know,
Where I'm allowed, or not meant to go??

If I go out for dinner I can't have a drink,
And I've to finish by 6, what on earth do they think?
That the virus doesn't come out until night?
How do they know that we'll all be alright?

I finally got myself back to the gym,
I loved it - the feeling of adrenaline,
But my fitness classes were no sooner started,
Restrictions were back and my fitness departed.

The "rule of six" what's that all about?
After 10pm we're not allowed out,
Only 2 households to mix at a time,
But the takeaway's open so we're going to be fine??

Encouraged if you can to work at home,
Using the internet and the telephone,
Face to face contact is done with a mask,
When the person is deaf this is quite a task!

If you're in my car you'll need to sit in the back,
As if covid won't always choose to attack?
If the radio's on please don't try to sing,
For fear you'll spread germs over everything!

If you go on holiday, be prepared.
Quarantine awaits because we're all so scared,
14 days until you're allowed back out,
Maybe the holiday we should've done without?

I can't go to the pub, bingo no more,
If I visit my friend I have to stand at the door,
Yet I can meet in a cafe where many can sit,
These rules are really a lot of S**t.

I can visit my granny in her lovely care home,
If I make an appointment on the telephone,
My extended household will be my Mum,
It was my brother before....so now it's her turn.

A 2nd lockdown looms in the air,
People flout the rules and really don't care,
I just pray that we'll all get through this alive,
And that in covid 19 - we all survived.

2 Years Down The Road

Are we post or mid-covid? Where are we actually at?
The news, it seems no longer fills in all the facts,
More interested in politics, it's left me quite confused,
Are we now in the stage where we can do whatever we choose?

We are learning to live with a virus that kills,
I had all my vaccinations, absolutely at will,
It's not catching covid itself that I fear,
I'm terrified of long -covid that then might appear.

I need my own routine for my mental health,
Long covid would give me fatigue in its stealth,
I couldn't do all the things that keep my head well,
Having no structure in my day feels like hell.

If I could be sure of covid being a 2 week spell,
Of feeling so poorly, feeling unwell,
I'd want to catch it to get it over and done,
But I see it impacts differently on everyone.

People tell me I'm silly to still feel so scared,
I can't help but panic like I'm so unprepared,
I' m doing my best to still carry on,
To live with the new virus of Omicron.

Angela McCrimmon

Emerging from Lockdown

We're following this roadmap with excitement in the air,
A year of being locked down, we are so very nearly there,
People ask if I am happy, assume I'm so relieved,
The truth is I'm terrified and I don't want to leave!

For me the last 12 months have brought a lot of peace,
Compared to "normal" life my anxiety decreased,
I haven't had to cope with getting out the door,
On days when staying at home would help me so much more.

I wake up with deep dread knowing the end is near,
I turn off the news because it's fueling all my fear,
Please don't misunderstand me, please don't get me wrong,
I want the world in safety, I want the virus gone.

It's just that in that safety by own comfort will dispel,
I'll be forced to face "normality" and I don't do that well,
While many have felt lonely and so isolated too,
But me?....I've felt an inner peace the whole way through.

I'd created a world within the world that really worked for me,
I thrived in many ways that were often plain to see,
Now I feel such panic and the reality of my fears,
Is driving me back to my bed each day in floods of tears.

So while the world starts to turn and for those who cannot wait,
Show some compassion for those who hesitate,
Mental health is complex and we all have a story to tell,
But for me coming OUT of lockdown is proving to be my hell.

The Pharmacy

Lockdown saw services step up and step out,
Always taken for granted but without a doubt,
On Pharmacists we realised we very much relied,
The stress they worked under is truly admired.

When we couldn't leave the house I'd see their vans,
Delivering medication as fast as they can,
Straight back to pharmacy to load up again
They were like one of those "Special Cargo" trains.

Prescriptions were changed with a sudden rise,
In anti-depressants and others like- wise,
Medication trays made, taken back to the start,
To add in another tablet to a new compart.

It wasn't long until the message received,
Was "Ask your pharmacist, not your GP,"
It's something I'd never thought of before,
And to be honest it filled me with dread even more!

Then one day things were awful and I had no choice,
I hadn't slept for weeks, I had to use my voice,
I spoke to him privately for fear I would cry,
I didn't want pity from any passers-by.

I'd never "consulted" my pharmacist before,
He was an enigma who worked the other side of the store,
Yet here I was with tears falling down on the table,
He was gentle and patient and above all, very stable.

He reassured me that I wasn't going totally insane,
There were many reasons my medicine wasn't working the same,
"It's what they mix it with...your liver destroys,
But we'll work together to find you a choice."

In effect I felt like I'd just seen my GP,
He was patient and caring, did his best to help me,
Where once I had feared his presence alone,
He told me anytime I could pick up the phone.

The pressure they were under we could never conceive,
Drugs being stuck and stopped overseas,
On occasion I had to pick something up from the chemist,
The respect they'd earned looked completely unblemished.

I'm sure there were bumps in the road on the way,
But they stepped up and stepped forward at the end of the day,
They were an essential service like never before,
When Covid 19 arrived at our door.

Angela McCrimmon

Gathering up the leaves of Lockdown

I gather up my thoughts as I reflect upon,
The time Covid stole, the minutes that are gone,
I gather my emotions, no chance to say goodbye,
Funerals online, so bizarre I couldn't cry.

I gather my gratitude as I very clearly see,
How powerful the last 2 years have been for me,
With Social Anxiety, Isolation was the key,
I gather the peacefulness I found inside of me.

I gather the memories of my rather manic phase,
My family and friends had to suffer me for days,
Days turned into weeks with the Dr's out of reach,
Gathering my reflections of the lessons that did teach.

I gather my growth as I learned about new things,
Determined to put my health at the top of everything,
I gather my sighs as I clearly can recall,
I'd created a new world with barely any stress at all.

I gather up my wisdom tho' it came at quite a cost,
I found out who my friends were and some I sadly lost,
Gathering connection as I finally found my Tribe,
Accepting every part of me and always by my side.

I gather the feelings that almost stopped my heart,
My stomach churned so fast and anxiety did start,
When all restrictions lifted I couldn't stop the tears,
Gathering up my terror and a million other fears.

I gathered all my courage knowing I had to face,
The new world we lived in, to somehow find my place,
I gathered what had served me well, leaving parts behind,
I'd learned so much about myself, about my fragile mind.

I gather up excitement seeing opportunities ahead,
Stepping out my comfort zone and slowing down my head,
I gather such compassion for anyone who hurt,
I'm aware that for some, "lockdown" really didn't work.

Most of all I gather the strength I found inside,
To re-enter the world when it was easier to hide,
I'm gathering all the memories, both the good and bad,
The strangest 2 years ever but they were the best I've ever had.

5
Family Forever

"Young woman, you will survive many near-deaths of your soul, but you must stand up, overcome your heart's wounds, rise from the ashes, and go on with your life – Alexandra Vasiliu

If ever there is something to remind you how precious life is, even on the days we don't appreciate that, it's losing your parents and realising your family has changed forever. I missed a lot of years with my Dad because he was unable to accept my Mental Health Condition in earlier years but I feel like we squeezed 12 years of memories into his last 12 months and when he left this world I know without any doubt how much love and respect we had for each other. My relationship with my Mum was different – like most mothers and daughters there was a point I'm sure she would have happily done Jail time for murder, but as I grew up and moved away we would keep in touch every day, many times a day. We truly were best friends and there wasn't anything I couldn't talk to her about. I deliberately tried to protect her from my mental health because I didn't want to cause her stress so there have been many hospital admissions I wouldn't tell her about until I had come out the other side but that was my desire to protect her, not her unacceptance of my illness. She was given one year to live and I moved in to take care of her but sadly God had other plans and took her much sooner. I'm heartbroken, but I'm relieved for my Mum that she didn't have to go through the same agonising cancer treatment that we watched my Father go through. There's also been another huge loss in my life that I don't talk about often but I wanted to let him know he is never forgotten and perhaps introduce him to some of you for the first time.

My Parents' biggest legacy is their children, Steven, Mark, and myself Angela, so it's up to us now to carry on in life and be the kind of people they'd be proud of. I could drown in sadness at having lost both parents or I can pick myself up and embrace life even more because yet again, I've witnessed it's fragility and that tomorrow is never promised. I choose the latter. Like we've all heard it said before….No matter how good or bad your life is, when you wake up in the morning be grateful that you still have one.

Words For My Dad

I've penned a hundred poems and I'm sung a million songs,
The one I didn't want to ever write is when you're gone,
Knowing our "Tomorrow's" will become our "Yesterdays,"
The beginning of goodbye to a Generation of the "Rae's."

Not all have had have a Father, a Daddy or a Dad,
At times you've been all 3, that's why I won't be sad,
Heartbroken yes, but I promise I will be strong,
I get that strength from you and have done all along.

Sometimes our roads were bumpy, and we felt misunderstood,
But our lives came back together in a way they only could,
I'm so lucky to be your daughter for girls can share their heart,
In a way that sons can't always do for fear the grief might start.

Memories of roller-skating holding hands with you,
I counted the days until Saturday, without a doubt I knew,
Each week I'd count the sleeps until I'd get my giant hug,
When I'd had a stressful week, you helped me to unplug.

I love you so much Dad and if I can help, please let me know,
There are no ends of the earth that for you I wouldn't go,
You were the first man in this whole world I ever loved,
It appears no-one compares and that's why I've got a dog. :)

You've given me many things and in return I promise you,
When unsure I'll pause and think "What would my Dad do?"
Of course sometimes the answer will definitely be, "NOT THAT!"
But mostly I'll seek your guidance, your compassion and your laugh.

I don't know how long you have but I know it isn't years,
I prefer to take it day by day but please forgive my tears,
My tears are just a message to say how much I care,
Forever and always Dad, In my heart you'll be right there.

Daddy and Daughter PhotoShoot

The courage of a dying man

Baby Angela with Daddy

Last photo taken together before he passed

The Courage Of A Dying Man

Where do you even start when you want to do your best,
To give someone the credit they deserve without contest,
A man I watched in awe for the last year of his life,
Determined to live each moment and fight, fight, fight!

We'd started off so hopeful, "About 7 years I would say,"
So he underwent the treatment so he could do his part half-way,
In time it was very evident, his condition did not respond,
This "acceptable" life expectancy suddenly now was gone.

He must have felt so crushed, but he was an Athelete at his core,
He played Squash for Scotland, No 1, and was adored,
So his mind had a discipline and a focus of very few,
A determination and a strength that kept him pulling through.

We had BBQ's in his garden, with family and friends,
He knew it might be the last time he'd see some of them,
His attitude was upbeat, no-one would realise just how ill,
Until everyone was gone, and he would have to lie so still.

We had a "Daddy and Daughter" photoshoot, we both had so much fun,
The photographer unaware of why we were having it done,
He had 6 months to live and I'd asked him if we could make,
A memory I could keep, that the cancer could not take.

We had an overnight hotel break, stayed up and talked all night,
We had a gentle swim, I prayed he would be alright,
The next day I followed him to a class they called Tai Chi,
I had an inside look at his world now, just my Dad and me.

His partner was turning 60, his body was growing tired,
By hell or high water he was determined to be right by her side,
He was so ill from the effects of such horrible, harsh, Chemo,
He danced with her at her party, so handsome in his tuxedo.

Not once did I hear him say "Why me?" His bravery every day,
Was inspirational and such testament to the late, great, John Rae,
He left us all with memories, I recall each one so clear,
Thanks to the courage of that dying man, his spirit is always here.

A Long Over-Due Conversation

A lifetime of rejection when it came to mental health,
Complete and utter repute for the hand that I'd been dealt,
A part out my armour, a real character defect,
I should "pull myself together," or words to that effect.

"Depression isn't real......look at everything you've got,"
"Wake up and smell the coffee boiling in the pot,"
He couldn't understand that my lows were not my choice,
I wasn't fighting hard enough were the words of which he'd voice.

We had love for each other but with an overhanging cloud,
He'd made it very clear that I shouldn't come around,
When I couldn't be the person he had taught to be so strong,
He couldn't handle my mental health if anything was wrong.

We lost a lot of years because he refused to believe,
That I wasn't in control of telling it to leave,
"Mind over Matter…" I'm a believer in that too,
But sometimes the "matter" is stronger than you.

Then one day an illness came knocking on his door,
The Father that I loved was invincible no more,
An athlete so strong and determined in his mind,
So sure there'd be an answer that only he could find.

We'd spend time together which led to many talks,
Like "Don't protect me Dad, I can handle what you've got!
I might have a mental illness but I get such strength from you,
I can handle what's ahead......and I'm always here for you."

From then there seemed no topic not open to debate,
Sometimes I'd stay overnight and we'd stay up talking late,
We'd talk about "real" things and sometimes he'd even cry,
So scared that people would think he somehow hadn't tried.

The illness was teaching him so many different things,
He started to find gratitude in the simple that life brings,
He'd lived a life of luxury and now realised the only wealth,
That had ever really mattered, was the one we call our health.

Facing terminal illness really softened up his heart,
I felt us pull together where before he pulled apart,
Being on his own rollercoaster helped him to realise,
That nobody would choose to live a life of lows and highs.

Throughout the many years my size would fluctuate,
Due to medications I was often gaining weight,

cont'd

My Father decried me and only saw a sloth,
"She has no self-control" is the attitude I got.

In the weeks near the end we were talking as we do,
He said "I'm sorry for being so harsh on you...
The weight gain...I get it....I'm getting bigger by the day,
And I know I'm barely eating, so it's side effects they say."

I looked at him sadly and I cuddled him that day,
"We're going to love you though this," was all that I could say,
But to realise that his illness was making him realise,
He'd misjudged me when he'd said I was all that he despised.

My mental health had always been such a huge taboo,
But suddenly he'd ask me, "so tell me, how are you?"
It was more than being "polite" he was asking me for real,
How was I *really* doing? How did I **really** feel?

With terminal illness it at least gave us some time,
To bring years of heartache back into align,
Apologies were made and relationships felt healed,
Conversations that seemed so insanely surreal.

I've loved my Dad every day of my whole life,
But it took his own illness, like a double edged knife,
Until he lost control and nature was cruel,
He held impossible standards and was nobody's fool.

It breaks my heart that he is no longer here,
But with my mental illness in the end I had no fear,
It took his own illness to open his eyes and see,
We don't choose to be ill, and he finally saw *me*.

Lost and Found

The pain has passed, the struggle faded,
Gone is the life that was degraded,
The soul was searched, and answers found,
Knowing no longer he'd be around.
The pain inflicted is now at peace,
The frustration and anger are all released,
The words that found a soothing place,
The kindness etched upon his face.
Determination to overcome,
Believing at times the fight was won,
So grateful for the Hospice care,
Reassuring and always there.
In time it was so clear to me,
I prayed that God would set you free,
This wasn't the life you thought you'd have,
Lost to cancer but I found my Dad.

What's An Anniversary?

What's an "Anniversary" when every day's the same?
The other 364 don't cause me lesser pain,
I could reminisce the hours of where we were last year,
But each memory just reminds me that you're no longer here.

So much has happened since we were last together,
It's only been one year but it feels like it's forever,
I'd give anything to have you here and with us "well,"
But I'm glad you're safe in heaven, far from this Covid hell.

I'm surrounded by your photos and see them every day,
I wear your tracksuit top - never thought I'd see the day,
When I'd fit into your clothing, albeit a little snug,
I wear the fabric on my skin as if I wear your hug.

We talk about you often, your stories make us smile,
As we realise that our versions can differ by a mile,
We remember favourite places or lyrics from a song,
We keep you in our hearts, right there where you belong.

I don't want my memory to get stuck on the past,
To cling in desperation to the time I held you last,
But the 2nd of November, by your bed, just after seven,
Is the day God broke our hearts when he took you up to heaven.

Dear Dad......

It's hard to believe it's now the 2nd year,
So many times I wished that you were here,
Times when I felt so alone and so sad,
I didn't want much but I wanted my Dad.

With the Medical Tribunal I finally had my say,
But I knew you were meant to be with me that day,
I let my tears fall when alone in my room,
It wasn't your fault that you left us too soon.

I tried to be brave and I kept it together,
I knew I'd get this one chance in forever,
The composure, the calm, the strength I displayed,
I'm just sorry Dad, for the price I have paid.

I think of you daily though people don't know,
I see reminders of you wherever I go,
Is it co-incidence or are you one step ahead?
Are you talking to me or is it all in my head?

I know that you'll know I was very unwell,
My world crashed down and with that I fell,
I lost my strength and all my hope died,
I called for you Dad, did you hear my cries?

I hope you're proud because I found my way through,
And I know full well that my strength is from you,
The determination that runs through my veins,
I get it from you because you're exactly the same.

I hope you're happy and your heart is at peace,
I know for sure that your pain was released,
I accept you are gone and I need never ask why,
For "Fathers and Daughters Never Say Goodbye."

Angela McCrimmon

Worst Fear Come True

For as long as I live I will never forget,
The day my very worst fear had been met,
My mother, in this world, my very best friend,
Cancer had struck and her life would soon end.

I sat still in shock as I tried to digest,
Fighting back tears, I was trying my best,
But how could I hear her awful fate spoken,
And not cry for my heart was so painfully broken.

I decided I needed to be on my own,
So I got in my car and drove back home,
I put my things down and just crawled into bed,
Crying so hard I had such a sore head.

I know this is life and we all have to go,
And there's almost a gift when you actually know,
Not suddenly gone with so much left unsaid,
With this illness I know it is different instead.

6-12months Doctors told my Mum,
How hard were those words to roll off her tongue,
To tell her children she doesn't have long,
I knew in my heart it's my turn to be strong.

I'll make sure there is laughter and fun in our days,
I'll take care of her needs in every which way,
I've bought a book called "Mum, tell me your life,"
She can dictate the words and we'll laugh as I write.

I want to gather each memory, both big and small,
She's my priority now and I'll give her my all,
But I must remember that I matter too,
I'll take care of myself because she'd want me to.

It's a privilege to be the one who can care,
Even when the time comes she won't know I am there,
She's my mother and forever my very best friend,
I'll keep her safe in my care until the very end

A Tribute To My Mum

I've experienced loss, but this is grief like no other,
When you say a final goodbye to your mother,
It's indescribable the depth of the pain,
Knowing that I'll never see her again.

She brought me into the world and there wasn't a day,
When she wasn't in my life, somehow, someway,
When I left home our relationship continued to grow,
And she became my best friend, it's so hard to let go.

It's no secret that I struggle with my mental health,
But I'm strong and I cope with the things I am dealt,
One way I cope is that I've trained my brain,
To find gratitude in life time and again.

I'm grateful for the special bond that we shared,
Though my heart is broken, in the end unprepared,
I'm so lucky for I know that regret has no place,
I showed her I loved her in so many ways.

We shared the same humour and would laugh our way,
Giggling like children throughout the whole day,
We shared holidays and always had such fun,
In some ways like a sister, though always my Mum.

We talked about so many things it is true,
Probably topics that might surprise you,
But that was the beauty, we could literally be,
Always authentic to such a degree.

I'm laughing when I think of my manic states,
I'd bounce through her door and she would tell me straight,
"You need to go, you'll make me insane!"
No offence taken as I bounced out again.

I loved our honesty, that we could be that real,
We respected each other and how we might feel,
On my low days if I had to cancel our plans,
She understood that it's just how I am.

I have so many memories and I know that with time,
Those memories will help heal this heart of mine,
But for now the tears will continue to come,
For with all of my being, I miss my Mum.

I've always known one day I would face this pain,
I've faced grief before and expected the same,
But losing my Mum is like nothing before,
It's like all of those griefs and then so much more.

Cont'd

Angela McCrimmon

They say that our hearing is the last thing we lose,
So I lay on her pillow and spoke to her too,
I thanked her for all the memories we made,
For nobody can ever take them away.

So how do I go on, when it's all said and done?
A new chapter that doesn't involve my Mum,
She will be in my heart and my thoughts every day,
My Mum, the beautiful, Mrs Joyce Rae.

Mum and me at one of my shows

Laughter with Mum

A picture of health

My little family

First My Daughter, Forever My Friend

Dear Angela,

I know there are times when you miss me so much,
But I'm right here beside you and I'm trying to touch,
Your heart and your memories to make you laugh,
For that's what we did - you're my other half.
I hear you when you cry because I'm lying right there,
I long to comfort you and tell you I care,
I couldn't do these things when I was alive,
But I'm different now, I've been healed and revived.
I know there's so much that you want to tell only me,
I'm still listening my child, it's just you can't see,
Each time you go to dial the telephone,
I feel your heart drop when you hear I'm not home.
I'm watching you follow all of your dreams,
Proud of you??? Girl, I could burst at the seams!
I'm so proud because you could have given up trying,
Consumed by your grief, like you're the one dying,
But I see what you're doing, you're holding life tight,
Making memories from dawn until the moonlight.
You're still creating the diamond art I adore,
I know this one's for me so I'll love it much more,
You say that you still hear my voice in your head,
Keep talking to me, it's just a little different instead.
I know that you've started singing again too,
And the Patient Role Play that I'd practice with you,
The drama that I begged you to give it a go,
My death gave you courage that you didn't know.
You're my little girl making her way all alone,
But when it's time, I'll be waiting to bring you back home.

Love, Mum xxx

Angela McCrimmon

The 3 Muskateers

It's a strange feeling when you realise both parents are gone,
It's like one day it hits you and before too long,
Anxiety asks, "What on earth will I do?"
I said a silent prayer and thanked God for you.

I thanked God for my brothers and for the love that we share,
One's in Australia but I still know he'd be there,
If ever I needed him although it's true he does struggle,
To know what to do in a psychological muddle!

My other brother is closer, 40 minutes by car,
We're more like best friends than siblings by far,
I can talk to him openly about Mum and Dad,
While my other brother still finds this a little too sad.

I feel so blessed to have these men in my life,
We all have different views on the after-life,
But we share the same view on taking care of each other,
Now that we have lost both our Father and Mother.

We are the biggest legacy that our parents could leave,
I try to keep this is mind as we continue to grieve,
The values instilled and our compassion for others,
Was drilled into us by our Father and Mother.

My Mum's approach to "honesty" was perhaps extreme,
But it was to balance my Dad's "lack of" it seems,
When young I felt the punishment didn't fit the crime,
But as an adult I reassured Mum, "We've turned out fine."

I feel so lucky I've shared this life with 2 others,
Protected for I'm still the "baby" of my brothers,
While I stand strong, proud and do my very best,
It's comforting to know, our love has stood the test.

Stood the test of childhood and all the screaming tears,
Stood the test of "Get OUT MY ROOM" for all those teenage years,
Stood the test of adulthood as we all chose different paths,
Now we've stood the test of losing both our Mum and our Dad.

I've always loved you both but somehow I love you more,
I feel part of me may have taken you for granted before,
But never have I been more relieved, more emotional too,
I'm so thankful to have brothers as special as you.

"Little Angels"....L-R, Mark, Angela, Steven

Friends as well as Family

My oldest brother Steven

My brother Mark

Silent Love

People think they know me but there's a part not many see,
I'm "open" about many things, but you're a private part of me,
Unless they've known my history, they are often unaware,
I wasn't always "single".....there was a time when you were there.

They don't realise I was married because I never say your name,
I'm sorry if that hurts you, please know I'm not ashamed,
I simply have accepted that at the age of 33,
God had to take you home, that's the way it had to be.

There's not a day goes by when you don't cross my mind,
I wonder if you're sad that you had to leave us all behind?
All the potential memories that your illness stole away,
But I'm grateful for the ones we made, as they will always stay.

Childhood sweethearts from the young age of 14,
We went separate ways then came back in between,
You were everything I wanted and needed, that is true,
I was just 10 years later in catching up with you.

My life was too flighty, you seemed too "grounded" for me,
Looking back in hindsight it's so clear for me to see,
You're exactly what I needed and our hearts remained together,
We were naive to take for granted that our lives would last forever.

I sometimes wonder if you're looking down, If you're watching me,
Would your heart be full of pride with everything you see?
Would you say "That's my wife," then radiate some love,
Straight from you to me that you could send me from above?

People make assumptions that I've been "single" all along,
They don't realise I was married and it's with you that I belong,
I don't feel the need to tell them, I don't want to open up that door,
It's such a sacred piece of "our" story... but David, I'll love you forever-more.

Photo taken on our first date at 16 and 14 years old, in a passport photo booth.

Last photo taken before David became ill

My Handsome Husband, age 20

Angela McCrimmon